W9-DBS-611

VISUAL™
Quick Tips

Sewing

VISUAL™
Quick Tips
Sewing

Visual®

by Debbie Colgrove

WILEY
Wiley Publishing, Inc.

Library of Congress Control Number: 2008923123

ISBN: 978-0-470-16565-2

Printed in the United States of America

10   9   8   7   6   5   4   3   2

Book production by Wiley Publishing, Inc. Composition Services

Praise for the VISUAL Series

I just had to let you and your company know how great I think your books are. I just purchased my third Visual book (my first two are dog-eared now!) and, once again, your product has surpassed my expectations. The expertise, thought, and effort that go into each book are obvious, and I sincerely appreciate your efforts. Keep up the wonderful work!

—Tracey Moore (Memphis, TN)

I have several books from the Visual series and have always found them to be valuable resources.

—Stephen P. Miller (Ballston Spa, NY)

Thank you for the wonderful books you produce. It wasn't until I was an adult that I discovered how I learn—visually. Although a few publishers out there claim to present the material visually, nothing compares to Visual books. I love the simple layout. Everything is easy to follow. And I understand the material! You really know the way I think and learn. Thanks so much!

—Stacey Han (Avondale, AZ)

Like a lot of other people, I understand things best when I see them visually. Your books really make learning easy and life more fun.

—John T. Frey (Cadillac, MI)

I am an avid fan of your Visual books. If I need to learn anything, I just buy one of your books and learn the topic in no time. Wonders! I have even trained my friends to give me Visual books as gifts.

—Illona Bergstrom (Aventura, FL)

I write to extend my thanks and appreciation for your books. They are clear, easy to follow, and straight to the point. Keep up the good work! I bought several of your books and they are just right! No regrets! I will always buy your books because they are the best.

—Seward Kollie (Dakar, Senegal)

Credits

Acquisitions Editor
Pam Mourouzis

Project Editor
Donna Wright

Copy Editor
Elizabeth Kuball

Technical Editor
Louise Beaman

Editorial Manager
Christina Stambaugh

Publisher
Cindy Kitchel

Vice President and Executive Publisher
Kathy Nebenhaus

Interior Design
Kathie Rickard
Elizabeth Brooks

Cover Design
José Almaguer

Photography
Matt Bowen

About the Author

Sewing has always been a part of who Debbie Colgrove is and what she does in her spare time. She started sewing with her mother as a youngster, taking her first tailoring class at age 14. Since 1997, Debbie has been the sewing guide for About.com and continues to build an extensive library of sewing information on the Web site. As the former Web editor for *Sew News* magazine, she traveled extensively meeting sewing enthusiasts from all over the United States. She enjoys introducing sewing to children and adults through teaching sewing classes and individuals at charitable organizations such as 4-H clubs and charity sewing nights. Debbie serves on her local Home Economics advisory board and also provides leader training for 4-H. She works with many sewing machine companies to keep the world abreast of the latest options available to home sewers. Debbie lives in upstate New York with her family.

Acknowledgments

After teaching many people to sew, I firmly believe that the book in your hands is the best possible learning tool for someone who wants to learn to sew. I can't thank the editors of this book enough for the opportunity to share the information that this book contains. I would also like to thank my husband and daughter for their patience and understanding when I lost track of time or deserted them.

I will never be able to thank my mother, Althea Triebel, for all the things she has done for me. But I would like to take this opportunity to thank her for teaching me to sew it correctly or rip it out (even when I balked) and for the endless hours of driving me to places to enhance my learning experiences.

Table of Contents

3

Hand Sewing

4

Fabric

Lining, Interfacing, and Stabilizers

Sewing Seams and Seam Finishes

Shaping Details

Edge Finishes and Facings

Zippers

Fasteners

Hemming Techniques

Using a Purchased Pattern

Adding Pizzazz

Problem Solving

Index   200

chapter 1

Getting to Know Your Sewing Machine

A sewing machine is the largest one-time investment you will make in sewing. Whether you buy a $10 sewing machine at a yard sale or spend thousands of dollars for a top-of-the-line machine that can do almost everything, it is important to know what you will need in a sewing machine before you go shopping. In this chapter, you'll learn some of the standard options that are available on sewing machines and how to prepare your machine for sewing.

New Sewing Machines

The price of new sewing machine is usually related to the durability of and the amount of options available on the machine. New sewing machines offer many options that are not available on machines you'll find at a yard sale. If you're in the market for a new machine, visit local dealers and ask questions before you buy.

The best way to learn about sewing machines is to visit sewing machine dealers and try different features on a variety of sewing machines. A yard-sale bargain may not be a bargain if the machine won't sew. Always ask to see a machine run before you buy it rather than risk ending up with disposal fees or repair expenses. Presser feet, power cords, and the manual for the machine will be an added cost if they aren't included with a used machine.

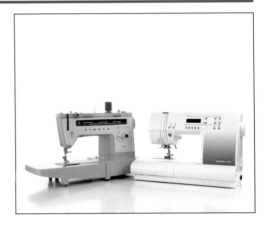

There is a huge variance in sewing machine prices. All sewing machine companies have upper- and lower-end machines. Many low-priced machines are considered "light-duty" machines, which means they're meant for mending or occasional sewing. Light-duty machines rarely hold up to everyday dependable sewing. Upper-end machines offer more options: the more you pay, the more options the machine is going to have. Take the time to learn about the options and weigh just how much you'd use the upper-end options.

FAQ

Why should I buy from a local dealer if I can find a better deal online?

Local sewing machine dealers offer lessons, usually free, with the purchase of a sewing machine. These classes are a great way to learn basic techniques and help you get the most from your sewing machine. Many dealers have sewing clubs and are knowledgeable about local sewing guilds. These clubs and guilds allow you to learn more and meet people who share a love of sewing. You won't receive these benefits from an online purchase.

Stitching Options

Every sewing machine has basic stitches, and those stitches should be strong and even. Upper-end machines also have many built-in decorative stitches. Rather than purchase a machine with a lot of stitch patterns you might not use, ask yourself how you will use those stitches.

UTILITY STITCHES

Basic utility stitches are the stitches that you're most apt to use every time you sew. **Straight stitches, zigzag stitches, stretch stitches,** and **blind stitch** or other hemming stitches are the most commonly used utility stitches. If you are shopping for a new sewing machine, don't be afraid to ask to see the available options and how or why you would use these stitches. The more you know, the more you'll experiment and become a happy customer—something all local dealers strive for in order to stay in business!

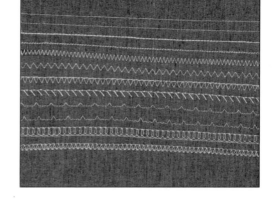

DECORATIVE STITCHES

How and where you might actually use decorative stitches requires honest analysis of what you'll be sewing. You can use decorative stitching to embellish or monogram.

Sewing decorative stitches and keeping them aligned evenly from an edge requires you to use guides on the sewing machine. When using a sewing guide, watch the guide rather than the needle.

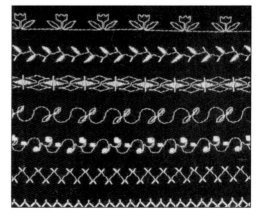

Sewing Machine Needles

The sewing machine needle is the most changeable and replaceable item on your sewing machine. Just as there are many different fabrics, you will need different sewing machine needles to sew those fabrics. Specialty sewing machine needles can help you get special effects that would not be possible with a standard needle. Check your sewing machine manual for the correct type of needle for your particular sewing machine.

NEEDLE SIZES

The size of the sewing machine needle is in direct correlation with the weight or thickness of the fabric you are sewing. Needles sizes are numbered using both European and American systems. Some companies label their needles with both systems, so you're apt to see 60/8 or 120/19 on a package. In both systems, the higher the number, the thicker the needle, and the larger the hole it will make in the fabric.

Needle Size Conversion Chart			
European	American	Fabric Weight	Fabric Examples
60	8	light	very sheer fabric
65	9	light	lightweight, see-through fabric
70	10	light-medium	light T-shirt fabric
75	11	medium	blouse fabric
80	12	medium-heavy	lightweight denim
90	14	heavy	corduroy, suiting
100	16	heavy	medium-weight denim
110	18	very heavy	jeans
120	19	very heavy	canvas

NEEDLE POINTS

Needles are available in **universal, sharp,** and **ballpoint** tips. The needles are designed for different types of fabrics. Your fabric may require a specific point type to obtain uniform stitching from your sewing machine. Universal-point needles can be used for sewing both knit and woven fabrics. Sharp needles are designed for woven fabrics. Ballpoint needles are designed for knit fabrics.

SPECIALTY NEEDLES

Topstitching needles have a larger than normal groove to accommodate thicker threads. They work very well for metallic thread that tends to shred with regular needles.

Stretch needles are the option for sewing knits when a ballpoint needle skips stitches.

Wing needles have a flared shank and are used to make decorative heirloom stitches.

Denim/jeans needles are designed for heavy fabric such as denim. The extra-sharp point is designed to penetrate layers of heavy fabric.

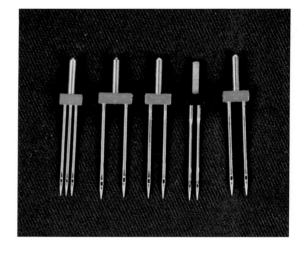

Double/triple needles (as shown above) are arranged on a crossbar with variable distances between the needles. Multiple upper threads are used with a single bobbin thread when sewing with a double or triple needle. These needles allow you to sew multiple lines of straight stitching that are parallel to each other.

Quilting needles are designed to sew through multiple layers and cross seams of quilts.

Self-threading needles are a perfect solution for someone who has difficulty threading a sewing machine needle. A tiny slit in the side of the needle allows the thread to pass into the eye of the needle.

Embroidery needles have a large eye and protect delicate decorative thread.

Needle position is usually controlled by the stitch width adjustment. The more positions that the needle can be placed in, the more accurately you'll be able to sew.

Stitch width is available on sewing machines that have zigzag capabilities. It adjusts the width of the stitches. When a change in the stitch width is used with a straight stitch, the position of the needle is changed from the normal center position.

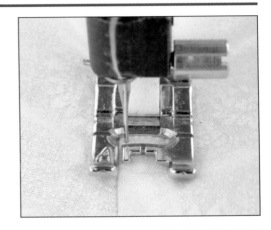

Being able to use the various parts of the presser foot as a guide while sewing, in conjunction with being able to change the needle position, allows you to keep your stitching straight and where you want the stitching to be. This is especially helpful in topstitching (see p. 152) and under-stitching (see p. 100).

Buttonhole Options

One of the most used options on a sewing machine is the buttonhole feature. For more information on the different types of buttonholes, see p. 132.

TYPES OF BUTTONHOLES

Not all buttonholes are created the same. Stretch fabric requires buttonholes that give with the fabric. Shank buttons may lay better with a keyhole buttonhole. The price of a sewing machine that can make every buttonhole imaginable is out of reach for most people, so you'll need to choose a machine with the buttonhole options that go with the buttons you'd like to use.

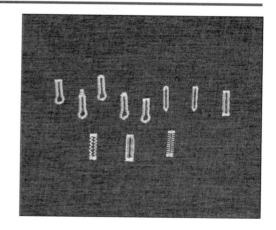

FOUR STEP VERSUS ONE STEP

Some sewing machines will have a four-step buttonhole option. To sew a four-step buttonhole, you have to stop and change the settings for all four sides of the buttonhole. Making identical buttonholes with this option requires concentration and accurate measurements. A sewing machine with a one-step buttonhole option will make the entire buttonhole in one continuous process automatically. Each buttonhole will be exactly the same as the previous one.

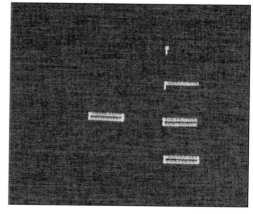

Sewing Machine Feet

Sewing machines have a basic presser foot that is adaptable to many sewing tasks. Newer sewing machines have snap-on feet, which are easily interchangeable. Specialty feet can expand the capabilities of your sewing machine and ease the completion of various tasks. Sewing machine dealers are the best resource for purchasing them.

Walking feet are special feet that feed the top layer of fabric the exact same way the feed dog feeds the lower layer of fabric.

Cording feet hold cording in place while sewing cording or corded pin tucks. The foot holds the cording and prevents it from wandering.

Darning feet allow you to do free-motion sewing. Free-motion sewing and quilting are techniques used for decorative quilting and artistic thread work.

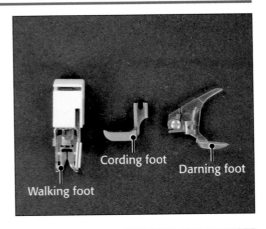

Cording foot

Darning foot

Walking foot

A **quarter-inch foot** is designed so that the edge of the foot is used as a guide to sew a perfect quarter-inch seam. This foot is especially helpful for piecing quilting.

A **ruffler** is a bulky foot that will automaticly gather and sew fabric in one step. Adjustments to various parts of the foot control the amount of gathering that is achieved.

A **rolled-hem foot** feeds the fabric, keeping it perfectly folded for a rolled or baby hem.

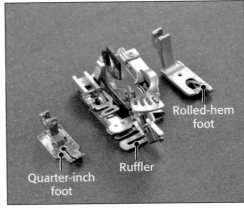

Rolled-hem foot

Quarter-inch foot

Ruffler

The Manual

When you purchase a new sewing machine, be sure to keep the manual because it will have all the information you need to operate your machine. No matter when your machine was manufactured, it will have variations from other machines, even those made in the same year. Take the time to read the manual and learn about everything your sewing machine has to offer.

If you don't have a copy of the manual or can't get one from the manufacturer of your sewing machine (see p. 198), you may be able to purchase one from one of the following sources. Be sure to have your machine's manufacturer and model number on hand when you're trying to track down a manual.

- **Shoppers Rule** sells manuals for more than 15 brands of sewing machines. To enlist its assistance with your machine brand and model number, write to Shoppers Rule at 2496 Starling Airport Rd., Arnold, MO 63010, call 800-636-3460 or 314-287-9640, or visit its Web site at www.shoppersrule.com.

- **Needlework Goodies and Other Neat Stuff** has a Web site with lists of manuals that are available in photocopy form via mail order. Visit www.needleworkgoodies.com and click on the link to sewing machine manuals.

Thread the Bobbin

The bobbin provides the underside thread for the sewing machine. Properly winding the bobbin is important to achieve the correct tension on the bobbin thread and have an acceptable stitch quality. The best source on how to thread your bobbin is the machine manual. (See the previous section or p. 198 if you don't have a manual.)

Most sewing machines wind the bobbin on the top of the machine before it is dropped in or placed in a bobbin case.

① Place the bobbin on the bobbin winder. Consult your manual for the correct type of bobbin to use.

② Place the thread spool in its position. Guide the thread to the one or two thread guides it must go through on its way to the bobbin.

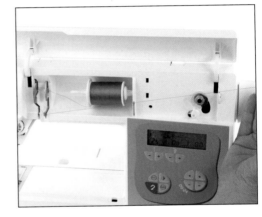

③ Manually wind the end of the thread around the bobbin a few times. If the bobbin has access holes in it, bring the end of the thread through one of the holes and wind it around the bobbin a few times.

④ Gently slide the bobbin holder over toward the bobbin-winding regulator or brake. See close-up of an already filled bobbin engaged against bobbin-winding regulator in the photo on the right.

⑤ Hold the end of the hand-wound thread and slowly engage the machine. Allow the machine to partially wind the bobbin, covering the entire shaft of the bobbin with two to three layers of thread. Trim the end-tail thread that you've been holding.

⑥ Keeping the machine speed slow and even, resume winding the bobbin until the sound of the machine changes or the bobbin stops turning because it has filled and is touching the bobbin-winding regulator or brake.

⑦ Slide the bobbin holder shaft and bobbin away from the bobbin-winding regulator or brake.

⑧ Place the bobbin in the machine as shown on the next page. Leave a long enough thread tail to thread the bobbin area.

Note: A small number of sewing machines have bobbins that wind in their final position. These machines with a bottom-winding bobbin usually have a button or latch that must be engaged for the bobbin to wind.

Place the Bobbin in the Sewing Machine

Bobbins are inserted in sewing machines in a variety of ways. Your machine manual is the best source for learning the proper way to insert the bobbin.

DROP-IN BOBBIN

Drop-in bobbins do not have a removable bobbin case. The bobbin is set in place. The bobbin tail thread is guided through necessary guides.

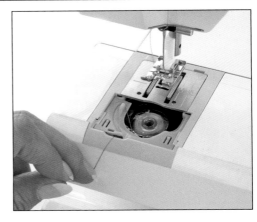

Once the sewing machine is threaded, the needle is lowered (see the first photo) and raised by turning the balance wheel to catch the bobbin thread and bring it through the throat plate as a loop of thread. Use a pin to unloop the thread, and pull it back under the presser foot (see the second photo). See p. 16–17 for threading the sewing machine.

REMOVABLE BOBBIN CASE

A large variety of sewing machines have a bobbin case. They mount differently from machine to machine. Most have a latch that releases the bobbin case from the machine.

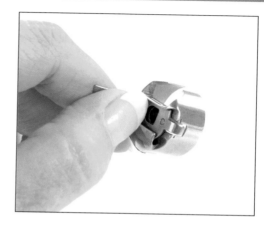

The bobbin tail thread is then threaded though the case slot and under the tension spring.

Hold the bobbin case by the latch (see above) to insert it back into the machine and follow the steps on the previous page for bringing the bobbin thread up through the throat plate.

Thread the Sewing Machine

All sewing machines vary slightly in how they're threaded. Your manual is the best resource for how to thread your machine. Your goal in threading the sewing machine is to get the thread from the spool to the machine needle, through all the guides so that the machine will sew even stitches.

Many older sewing machines have a threading diagram inside the end of the machine.

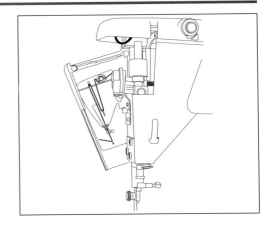

New sewing machines may have threading diagram arrows on the machine to follow as you thread the machine.

The following steps are general instructions for threading a sewing machine.

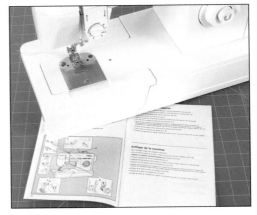

1. Place the machine presser foot up. When the presser foot is down, the tension discs are engaged, and the thread will not sit properly in the tension discs with the foot down.

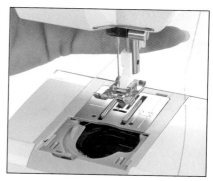

2. Place the thread on the sewing machine. Thread is held on the spool holder. Spool holders come in assorted varieties. Horizontally built-in spool holders also have a vertical spool holder option. Use the appropriate spool holder for your spool of thread.

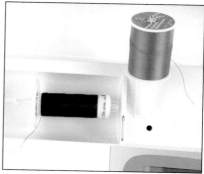

3. The next step is usually a thread guide. Thread guides come in various shapes and forms. It may be a hook design or a button design. Drawing thread from the spool, run the thread to the thread guide, which is closest to the spool of thread.

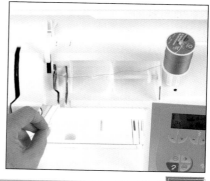

④ Watch for another thread guide as you move the thread downward to the tension discs. Slide the thread into the tension disc and upward.

⑤ Guide the thread upward to the take-up lever. The take-up lever may have a slot in it to slide the thread in, or you may have to thread it like a needle eye.

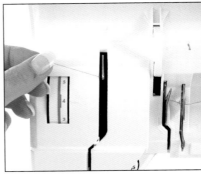

⑥ Once you have the thread through the take-up lever, guide it downward toward the needle. There are usually two thread guides before the thread goes to the needle. One may be on the front of the machine, and one is just under the machine body, almost hidden if you aren't looking for it.

7 Guide the thread to the needle. Just above the needle, there is usually a guide you must take the thread through.

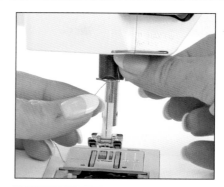

8 Thread the needle, and place the thread tail under the presser foot toward the back of the machine.

9 Thread the bobbin and bring the bobbin thread up through the throat plate. See p. 14.

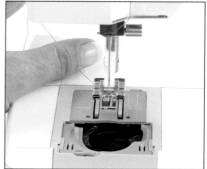

10 Test the stitching on a scrap of fabric.

chapter 2

Getting Ready to Sew

Having the correct tools will help you achieve professional-looking results. Collecting the basics doesn't have to break the bank. As your experience grows, you'll always find new tools and techniques that will make any sewing job easier.

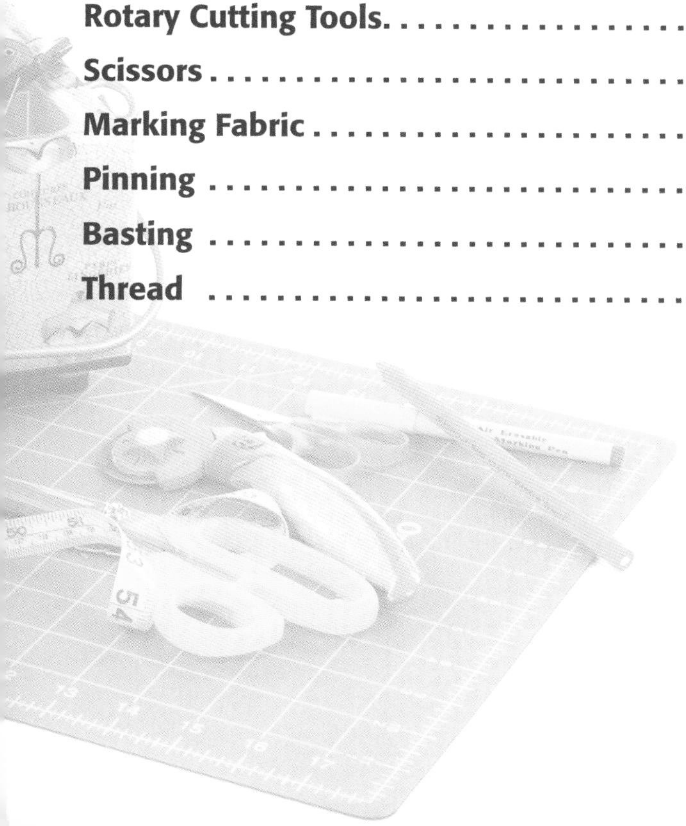

A sewing box can be as simple as a plastic container or as fancy as an expensive sewing box. Having a place to keep your sewing tools keeps the tools at hand for sewing and prevents them from being picked up and used impulsively for tasks that may dull sewing tools.

- **Cutting tools:** Your sewing box should include sharp dress-maker shears or scissors, nippers, and/or embroidery scissors, which are dedicated to sewing. They must be sharp and reserved for only cutting fabric and thread.

- **Pins and needles:** You should have different sizes on hand that are sturdy enough to not bend through heavy fabric and small enough to not leave holes in fine, lightweight fabric.

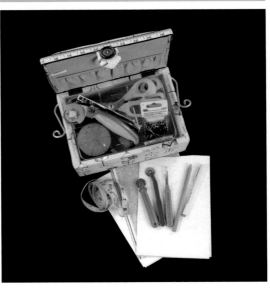

- **Marking tools:** Dress-maker's carbon, marking pencils, and vanishing pens can be used as needed.

- **Seam ripper:** No one is perfect, and stitches sometimes need to be removed. A seam ripper is used to cut one stitch at a time. The thread is removed by lifting the thread from the fabric.

- **Needle threader:** This inexpensive gadget has a wire that easily passes through the eye of the needle. The thread then goes through the wire, and the needle threader is pulled back out of the eye of the needle, bringing the thread through the eye at the same time.

Rotary cutting tools were designed for quilters but are great tools for many other sewing tasks. Rotary tools allow you to cut long straight lengths for things like ruffles and bias tape as well as quilting squares. The rulers provide an accurate way to measure the grain-line markings on patterns across a wider area than a gauge or tape measure. This increases your accuracy in evenly placing a pattern piece from the selvedge or fold of the fabric.

Rotary cutters are designed to glide right next to the edge of rotary rulers. The thin, very sharp, circular blade promotes fast, accurate cutting.

Rotary cutting mats are self-healing. Use a rotary cutting mat with a rotary cutter so that neither your blade or work surface are damaged.

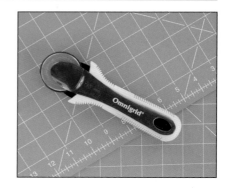

Rotary rulers have repeated measure-ment markings that allow you to line up the markings with two edges at the same time to achieve perfect angles and straight edges as shown in the photo on the right. The 6- x 24-inch ruler is well suited for measuring grain lines while laying out pattern pieces.

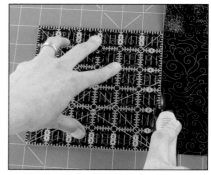

TIP

Limited Budget
If you have a limited budget for sewing tools, sign up for fabric store mailing lists to receive coupons and sales notifications. Look for frequent buyer programs and clubs to receive discounts.

Sharp scissors cut through fabric without shredding and tearing the fabric. The sharper the scissors are, the more accurate your cutting will be.

Dressmaker sheers (1) are a must for cutting out patterns. When cutting fabric, the long straight blade stays flat on the cutting surface.

Nippers (2) and **embroidery scissors** (3) are for cutting threads. Their compact size helps prevent accidental cuts in fabric.

Pinking shears (4) have a saw-tooth blade. The cut edge left by pinking sheers can be used as a seam finish on fabric that is only slightly prone to fraying.

Appliqué scissors (5) have one blade that is large and flat, which lies on the lower fabric while you trim away an appliqué. It protects the lower fabric from being cut accidentally.

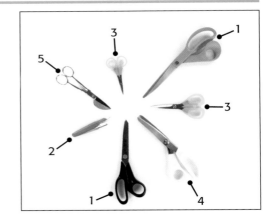

TIP

Keep Them Sharp

Using scissors to cut paper dulls the blades. Even a cheap pair of scissors will stay sharp longer if you don't cut paper with them. Label paper scissors and fabric scissors to avoid using them on the wrong materials.

In order for a pattern to be sewn in the way it is pictured on a pattern envelope, you have to sew the pattern accurately. Pattern markings guide you in joining the fabric. Darts, button placement, and dot markings all need to be transferred from the pattern to the fabric. This can be done using one of the three methods below.

To test which marking method will work the best, use fabric scraps from your project. Make sure the markings don't show through to the right side of the fabric and that the markings will wash out of the fabric.

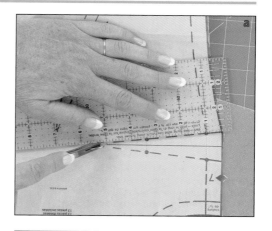

- Keep the pattern in place, and remove only as many pins as necessary to mark the fabric. Use **dressmaker's carbon** and a **tracing wheel** (a) with a straight edge to transfer lines and guides. Mark the wrong side of the fabric with a carbon color that varies from the fabric just enough for it to be visible.

- Place a pin through the pattern markings, and mark the fabric with **tailor's chalk** or **tailor's pencils** on the wrong side of the fabric.

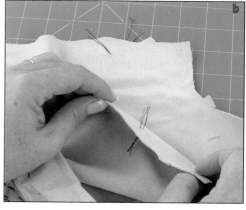

- **Tailor tacks** (b) are loops of thread that are sewn through pattern markings to transfer those markings to delicate and napped fabric. The layers of fabric are gently separated, and the loops are cut to leave thread strands in the fabric.

Pinning is a fast way to temporarily hold the fabric where it needs to be while you sew it in place. Keep the fabric smooth and the pins out of the way of the sewing machine needle.

Position the fabric layers and weave the pin into and out of the fabric with the point of the pin toward the area you'll be sewing. Never place pins in the line you'll be sewing.

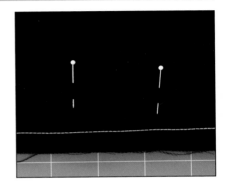

Use pins to align dots on a pattern by placing the pin in one dot and then the dot on the other side before weaving the pin back into the fabric. Pinning the fabric will temporarily hold it in place for you to baste (see next page). Always remove the pins before sewing at the sewing machine or remove the pins as you approach them. The needle might break if it hits a pin

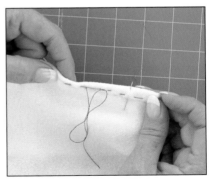

TIP

Pinning Delicate Fabric

Pins can leave holes and snags in delicate fabrics. Try silk pins and pin in seam allowances whenever possible to avoid damaging the visible side of the fabric.

Basting

Basting is long stitches that can be easily removed. It is used to temporarily hold fabric together before final stitches are sewn.

Always sew basting stitches next to but not exactly where you will be sewing the final stitches. Final stitches over the basting can make them difficult to remove, and the fibers from the basting thread might be visible in your final stitching. For more on hand basting, see p. 35.

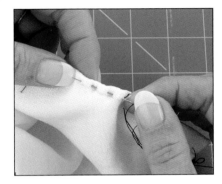

Machine basting is sewn with the longest straight stitch your machine will sew.

Basting for a zipper is done with the regular seam allowance to temporarily hold the seam perfectly aligned. Backstitch the regular seam before starting the basted area.

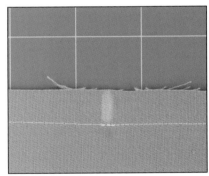

FAQ

Should I backstitch my basting stitches?

Backstitching is done to lock the stitching and prevent the stitches from coming out. Because you want to be able to easily remove basting stitches, you usually won't backstitch when sewing basting stitches.

Thread comes in a wide variety of colors, as well as a variety of fibers and weights. Try not to buy thread just because it's pretty.

All-purpose thread is used for almost any general sewing task. Cotton and polyester thread is the most readily available. If you are sewing with cotton fabrics (as in quilting), you should sew with cotton thread.

Thread quality will make a difference in the way your machine functions and the strength of your seams. Bargain-bin thread is not a bargain if a seam comes undone or your machine will not sew properly.

Furthermore, inexpensive thread may be more susceptible to shrinking, which can lead to puckered seams after one washing. Protect your time investment by spending a bit more on quality thread to avoid shrinking thread.

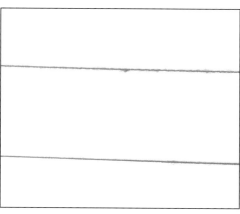

Due to variations in the U.S. and European thread weight labeling system, seeing and touching the thread is your best bet. Use lighter, thinner weight thread for lightweight fabrics and heavier, thicker weight thread for heavier fabric.

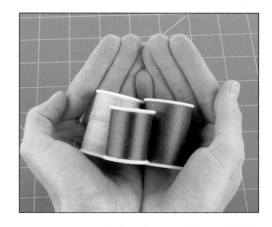

Choose thread color to match the background or predominant color on the right side of the fabric. When an exact match is not available, choose a slightly darker color thread as thread sews in one shade lighter.

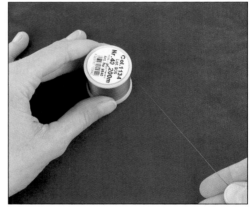

FAQ

Does thread age?

Thread does age. Test thread before you use it by stretching a length of it between both hands. If it breaks easily, it will break easily in the garment. Store thread out of direct sunlight and dusty environments to preserve its original quality.

chapter 3

Hand Sewing

Many things cannot be sewn by machine, and even if the machine can sew it, hand stitching will, in some instances, give you a better finished result. Hand sewing allows you to have control over hiding stitches when you sew hems and many types of fasteners. Secure stitches are necessary to hold fasteners in place and to have sewing that will hold up to laundering.

For many people, threading a needle is the biggest challenge there is in hand sewing. It doesn't have to be! There are gadgets and tricks to get the job done easily without breaking a sweat.

① Cut the end of the thread at an angle with sharp scissors.

② Using a needle threader, push the wire of a needle threader through the eye of the needle. Insert the end of the thread into the wire loop. Then pull the wire loop and thread back out of the eye of the needle.

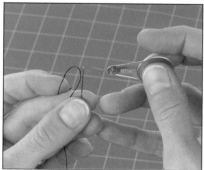

TIP

Floppy Thread

Thread that is limp can be difficult to guide through the eye of the needle. Coat the thread with beeswax (available in notions departments) to give it enough stiffness to control the thread.

Working with a double threaded needle may seem easier to use than a single threaded needle, but it may not give you desirable results.

Use a single thread whenever you want the stitching to be as invisible as possible and when you want to create as little bulk as possible.

Always keep the thread doubled near the needle and single in the area where the thread is being consumed by sewing. Gently pull the thread through the needle after every few inches of sewing to move the double thread area up toward the needle.

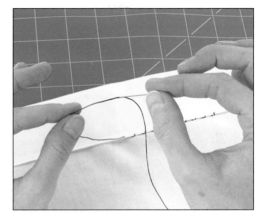

A double thread is used when you want strong, durable stitches. Sewing on buttons or fasteners is typically done with a double thread. When sewing with a double thread, both ends of the thread are the same length and knotted together.

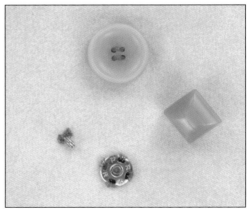

The knot on hand-sewing thread should be at the end of the thread without a tail of thread beyond the knot. The size of the knot depends on the weave and weight of the fabric you're sewing. A heavy, loosely woven tweed fabric will need a large knot, while a thin, silky fabric will require a small, fine knot.

1 Place the end of the thread on the palm side of your index finger, with the end of the thread toward your body. Hold it in place with your thumb.

2 Bring the thread under your index finger, around your finger until it will slip under your thumb.

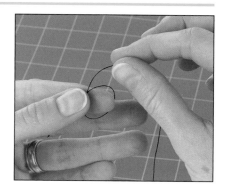

3 Roll the thread between your thumb and index finger, while rolling across the bottom of your thumb.

4 Allow the end of your middle finger to help hold the thread between the bottom of your middle finger and the top of your index finger. Pull the thread with your right hand as you use your thumbnail and index finger to snug the knot down to the end of the thread.

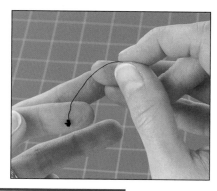

TIP

A Large Knot
You can make a large knot by rolling the thread more on your finger or by repeating the entire procedure and encapsulating the first knot.

Hand basting is the best way to hold fabric together to keep it from sliding or to test the fit before sewing permanent stitches. Hand basting should also be easy to remove. A running stitch is the fastest and easiest way to baste.

1. Thread a needle to sew with a single thread and knot the end.

2. Sew an anchor stitch which will anchor the knot in the seam allowance.

3. Insert the needle next to the seam line and through both layers of fabric. Do not place the needle directly on the seam line so you can avoid machine sewing over the basting. This will make the basting stitches easy to remove.

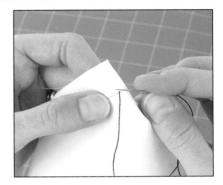

4. Using long, uniform stitches, weave the needle in and out of the fabric to hold the fabric in place.

   Note: Small evenly placed running stitches commonly replace machine stitching on hand sewn fine delicate seam work.

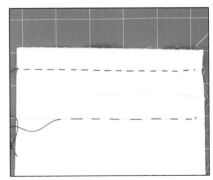

TIP

Washable Basting
You can use a washable glue stick on washable fabric to temporarily "baste" fabric in place. Always test the glue and its washability on a scrap of fabric before using it on your project.

A backstitch is a strong durable stitch that can replace machine stitching. It can be used for mending or construction.

①　Sew an anchor stitch in the seam allowance or an unseen area on the wrong side of the fabric.

②　Insert the needle up through the fabric on the seam line.

③　Push the needle down through the fabric behind the first stitch, and bring the needle up in front of the first stitch.

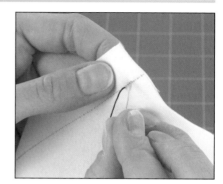

④　Insert the needle down behind where the needle came up, butting up to the end of the previous stitch. Repeat until you have sewn the desired area.

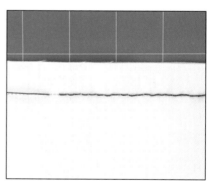

TIP

Needle Size

The size of the needle you choose to do hand sewing is chosen for fineness of a stitch and the weight of the fabric you're sewing—not because the needle has a large eye and is easy to thread.

A slipstitch is a popular hemming stitch. It's visible on the inside and barely visible on the outside. Tacking facings and cuffs are other examples of when a slipstitch would be used.

1 Anchor the knot in an inside edge.

2 Take a tiny stitch in the body of the garment, picking up just a few threads of the fabric, opposite from where you anchored the knot.

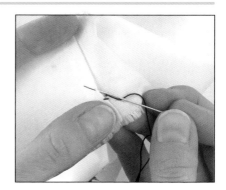

3 Bring the needle back to the inside area (hem or facing), approximately a quarter inch from the stitch in the fabric, and anchor the thread with a stitch. Repeat until you have sewn the desired area.

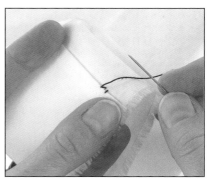

TIP

Keeping It Invisible
Use a single thread and pick up as few threads of the outside fabric as possible to keep your stitches invisible on the right side.

Catch-Stitch

The catch-stitch is a very strong hemming stitch. It is a great stitch to use in hems that could get caught in heels or have unusual stress put on them. Unlike other hand stitches, a catch-stitch is sewn from left to right.

1 Hide the knot inside the hem edge, bringing the needle out in the edge of the hem.

2 Move approximately a quarter inch to the right of where your previous stitch was formed, and make a small horizontal stitch that only picks up a few threads of the fabric, inserting your needle from right to left.

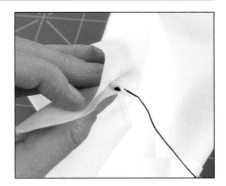

3 Pull the needle through the fabric and make the exact same stitch in the outside of the hem forming X shaped stitches; repeat until you've finished the hem.

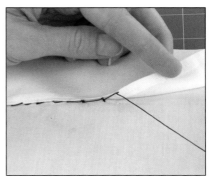

TIP

Time Saving

Save your hand sewing for watching television, waiting in doctors' offices, or waiting in the car while your kids finish soccer practice. Pack it in a tote bag with needle and thread so you have it ready to sew when you have time that would be wasted otherwise.

Blind Stitch

A blind stitch is a hidden stitch that can only be found by pulling back the fabric to find the stitching. It's sewn with a catch-stitch or slipstitch, away from the edge of the hem, which prevents the edge of the hem from "denting" the fabric. This is especially important when using bulky fabrics.

① Fold the body of the garment back on itself, right sides together, to meet the inside edge of the hem. Do not press the body of the hem back—just give it a gentle rollback so that you can keep the hand stitching directly across from the stitches you'll be making on the hem.

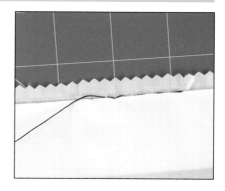

② As you stitch from the right to the left, catch just a couple of threads of the fabric on the body of the garment and on the hem. Your goal is to have as little stitching as possible show on the inside and on the outside of the garment while the stitching holds the hem in place.

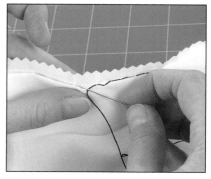

TIP

Thick Fabric

Hiding hem stitches made in heavy fabric is easy when you guide the thread through the fibers rather than between the fibers that makes up the fabric.

A chain stitch is a decorative stitch used for embellishment. It is made with a series of loops.

① Anchor the knot on the wrong side of the fabric, bringing the needle to the right side of the fabric. Insert the needle right next to where you came up through the fabric, and bring the needle point back up to the right side of the fabric, ⅛ to ¼ inch in front of where you went into the fabric.

② Loop the thread over the top of the needle and down around the needle to the bottom of the needle to form a loop.

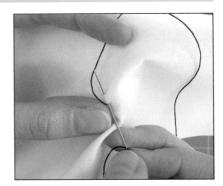

③ Pull the needle up through the fabric and the loop.

④ Place the point of the needle into the fabric, just inside the top of the formed loop and repeat, making another loop. Repeat until you have the desired amount of chain stitching.

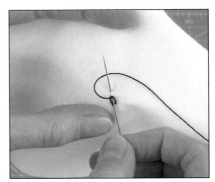

TIP

Embellish Appliqués

A chain stitch allows you to add enhancing lines and dimension to appliqués. Use embroidery thread and single or multiple lines of chain stitching to add stems to flower appliqués.

Thread Chains

Thread chains can be used for a button closure, to create delicate belt loops, or as an eye for a hook-and-eye–type closure. A small thread chain is also used to help lining stay aligned at seams. The chain itself is made with "finger crocheting".

1 Anchor the thread on the back side of the garment or in a seam allowance, bringing the needle to the surface. Sew one chain stitch where your needle came through the fabric, but hold the loop with your fingers.

2 Pull the needle thread through the loop, holding the loop in your fingers.

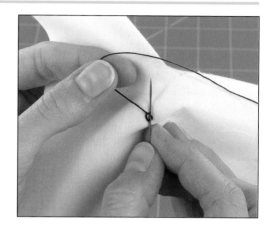

3 Repeat until you have the desired amount of thread chain. Pull the needle and thread through the last loop.

4 Anchor the thread chain in the fabric at the desired position using a backstitch.

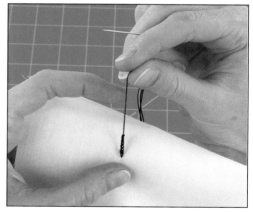

Many higher-end sewing machines have a built-in buttonhole or blanket stitch, but sewing in small areas and being able to adjust the size of the stitch makes hand sewing this stitch a viable option. A buttonhole stitch is sewn so that the stitches are exactly next to the previous stitch. This way, the entire raw edge of the buttonhole is covered with thread.

① Anchor the knot on the wrong side of the fabric. Insert the needle in the same spot that you hide the knot, bringing the point of the needle to the edge of the sewing area and through a loop of the thread as shown in the photo on the right.

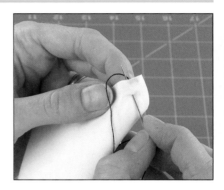

② Insert the needle ½ inch or the desired distance from the first stitch and repeat, bringing the needle through the loop.

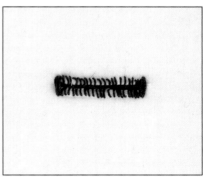

TIP
You can use this stitch with yarn to cover the edge of a single-cut piece of fleece fabric to create a blanket.

If your hand sewing comes undone, the way you end your stitching may be the culprit.

① Find a spot that will not show at the end of the area where you were sewing, and sew a backstitch (see p. 36). Repeat another backstitch wrapping the thread under the needle as shown.

② Move over from your first backstitches and repeat, creating two more backstitches. Cut the thread.

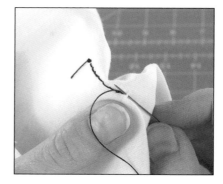

Note: *On a fine fabric where multiple backstitching could leave too much thread visible, work a chain stitch to make a small knot.*

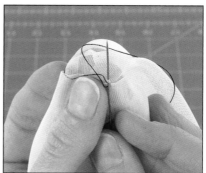

TIP

Secure Without Adding Bulk

When you're ending your hand stitching, do not backstitch more than twice in the same spot. Move your ending stitch over just a little so that you don't create bulky, knotted stitching in one spot.

chapter 4

Fabric

Strolling through a fabric store is an adventure in imagination. The array of fabric colors and textures are a smorgasbord of raw material ready to be made into anything you can imagine. If you enter a fabric store with a specific project in mind, it is best to know how that the fabric will sew and appear in your finished product before you make your purchase and invest your time.

Choosing a piece of fabric is not as simple as finding a fabric that you love at first sight. The fabric needs to be suitable for your particular project. The type of fabric you use can affect how a finished item will hang or drape.

Most quilting stores and fabric stores carry **100 percent cotton** in a wide variety of colors and prints. This type of fabric tends to stay in place when it lies against itself, making it one of the easiest fabrics to sew.

Aside from 100 percent cotton, other blends of **woven fabric** are a good choice for beginner sewers. Woven fabrics are available in a variety of weights from fine sheer fabric to heavy upholstery and canvas fabric.

Polar fleece is a great fabric to experiment with. It does not fray, so seam finishes are not necessary. It's available in a wide variety of weights, colors, and patterns as shown in the photo on the right.

Slippery fabrics, such as satins, sheers, and Lycra, as well as super-stretchy fabrics, require a bit of experience to achieve desirable results.

Fabric is sold in precut flats or off a bolt by the yard (or by the meter in some countries). Buying a fraction of a yard is perfectly acceptable so you can buy only the amount of fabric you need.

Before you buy fabric, you'll need to know how much fabric your pattern requires, and you may need extra fabric if you're adding length or width to the pattern. You'll also need to allow for enough fabric in case the fabric shrinks.

Use this handy chart when you need to buy less than a yard of fabric.

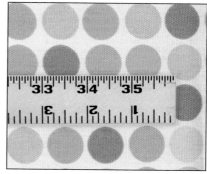

Yards	Inches
⅛ yd.	4½"
¼ yd.	9"
⅓ yd.	12"
½ yd.	18"

Yards	Inches
⅝ yd.	22½"
⅔ yd.	24"
¾ yd.	27"
1 yd.	36"

TIP

Fat Quarters

Many stores have precut fat quarters and fat eighths. These pieces are ¼ or ⅛ of a yard but are not cut in the conventional method. A ½ or ¼ yard is cut from a full width of the fabric and then that piece is cut in half. This leaves two pieces of fabric, which are sold individually as a *fat*. Although this cutting method was developed for quilters, these fat cuts are an excellent way to have a stash of many colorful pieces of fabric to experiment with different sewing techniques such as appliqué.

Unless it is a remnant or a precut flat, fabric is usually folded and wrapped on cardboard as a *bolt* of fabric. The end of the bolt has a label that gives you the information you need to make an educated purchase. Unfolded fabric that is wrapped around a tube will have a hangtag or sticker on one end with the same information you would find on the bolt label. Be sure to write down this information, and keep it with your fabric just in case you need to buy more.

The bolt label will contain care information on the proper way to clean and dry the fabric. Dry cleaning, cool or warm water washing, and machine drying are just a few of the options you might find for fabric care.

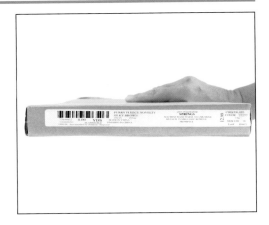

The fabric manufacturer and the style number and/or name will also be on the bolt end. This information is extremely helpful when shopping for the best prices, either online or in fabric stores.

The bolt label will also contain information on fiber content, which may be important if you have allergies or sensitive skin. If your fabric is a remnant or you don't have the bolt end information, see p. 199 to learn how to determine your fabric's fiber content.

All fabric has a selvedge. The *selvedge* is the bound area of the fabric on the uncut edges. If you find fabric that is cut on all edges, chances are that it is a remnant and was originally from a fabric bolt or tube. Not every selvedge is the same; some are plain and some offer information.

Print repeat marks can be found on the selvedge (a). These will allow you to calculate how much extra fabric you'll need if you're matching a repeated pattern in the fabric.

Color dots or blocks on the selvedge show you each color that is in the print of the fabric, making it easier to pick out and match a single color from a print (b).

The manufacturer's name may be found on the selvedge but you will not find as much information on the selvedge as you will on the bolt end.

a   b

TIP

Cut It Off!
Always cut the selvedge off the fabric before you begin your project. It may be tempting to use that extra little bit of fabric, but the selvedge tends to launder and shrink differently than the rest of the fabric.

Fabric grain is the way the threads (or fibers) that make up the fabric travel. If you've ever had a pair of jeans that wanted to twist or wrap around your leg instead of hang straight, you've experienced why cutting fabric on the straight grain is important—that twisting, wrapping jeans leg was not cut on the straight grain.

Lengthwise grain runs horizontally to the selvedge or the length of the fabric. Lengthwise grain is usually used to run the length of a garment (a).

Crosswise grain runs perpendicular to the lengthwise grain. Crosswise grain runs across or around a garment (b).

Bias grain is the grain that runs at a 45-degree angle to the straight grains of the fabric (c). Bias grain will hang differently and has stretch even on a woven, non-stretch fabric.

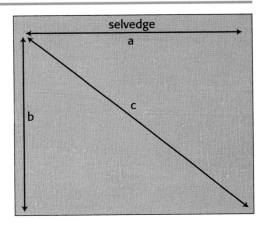

The photo on the right shows how fabric will stretch on the bias.

It can happen! You may get a piece of fabric where the cut end has not been cut on the straight grain. The important thing is that you'll need to fix the grain before you cut out the pattern pieces so that the pieces are truly cut on the straight grain.

1 After the fabric has been preshrunk, snip an edge of the selvedge near the raw, cut end of the fabric.

2 Rip cotton fabric across the raw edge, using the snip as a starting point. Refold the fabric as it came off the bolt, matching the selvedges and the newly ripped edge to themselves.

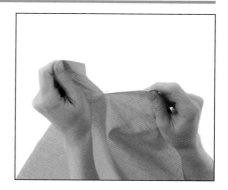

3 If the "fold" is not lying straight and smooth, the fabric is off grain. Unfold the fabric and pull from opposite corners of the fabric, as you would a free-standing frame to pull the threads into alignment. Repeat until the fold does lie properly.

TIP

Look Before You Buy!

Striped fabric needs the stripes to be printed on the straight grain. Before you buy, look closely at the threads of the fabric for a continuous thread to follow a stripe.

Most fabrics are either woven or knitted. Because all knits have stretch, a woven fabric is the best choice for beginners to use to learn to sew and for experienced sewers to test-drive a new sewing machine. In general, woven fabrics are less likely to have distorted results because they don't stretch.

Woven fabric is composed of threads running horizontally and vertically, weaving in and out to form the fabric.

Knit fabric is composed of threads that form loops. These loops allow the fabric to stretch.

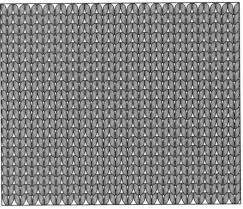

Fabric Nap and One-Way Designs

Fabric nap is not that the fabric needs to take a snooze! Fabric printed with one-way designs and fabric with nap need all of the pieces to be cut in one direction.

Nap is the way the pile of the fabric lays. Fabrics such as velvet, velour, and corduroy are fabrics with nap. If the fabric looks like a different shade from different angles, it must be handled as fabric with nap.

One-way designs are prints that need to be cut facing in one direction. For example, a print with chairs on it, as shown on the right, would need to be cut out so that the chairs are oriented with the chair legs down.

TIP

Exceptions to the Rule

Any fabric can be an exception to the rule. Fold and place the fabric on a tabletop so that you can see it from both directions and step back. If you see any difference in the two directions, use the with-nap cutting layout in the pattern directions.

Aside from their beauty, lace and sheer fabric offer dimension, texture, and elegance to a sewing project. The new glitz and glitter sheers and netting can make projects more appealing to the eye.

Watch for large lace patterns that may create awkward seams. Fold back two sections of the lace and see if joining them will be acceptable with normal sewing methods, and without advanced cutting work.

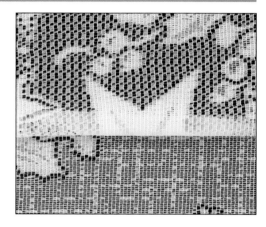

Enhanced sheers are available with glitz, glitter, iridescence, and prints. Always test the appearance of the fabric from two directions to see if a with-nap cutting layout will be needed (see the tip on the previous page).

Preshrink Fabric and Notions

Preshrinking washable fabric and notions that will be used in a sewing project is essential to having a finished item that can be laundered with confidence.

1. Before you preshrink fabric, secure the raw cut edges of the fabric with a zigzag stitch to prevent fraying.

2. Launder the fabric according to the end of the bolt care instructions or how you intend to launder the finished item.

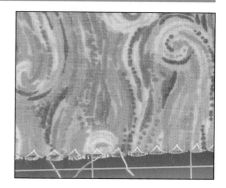

3. Launder and dry the notions such as zippers, bias tape, trims, and lace the same way you will be laundering the finished item. A lingerie bag or stocking is a great way to prevent these items from being tangled while they are laundered.

4. Press, straighten, and smooth the fabric and notions after they have dried.

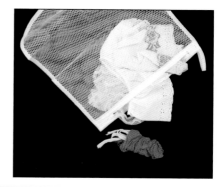

FAQ

Why did my fabric fade when I preshrunk it?

Fading can happen to any fabric, particularly dark fabrics with excessive dye. Preshrinking the fabric allows it to happen before you have invested the time and energy into sewing the fabric.

chapter 5

Lining, Interfacing, and Stabilizers

Lining, interlining, stabilizers, and interfacing are all inside elements of a project and are rarely seen. So why do they make a difference? The choices you make for the inside of a sewing project will affect the way the outside will stand up or drape; it impacts the overall appearance. This chapter will help you make the appropriate choice for any sewing project.

When you know the definitions of what is needed inside a sewing project, you can ask for those products in a fabric store or search for them online. This will increase the likelihood that you'll purchase exactly what you need.

Lining is sewn separately and joined inside an identically sewn item. A man's suit jacket, a handbag, or a lined skirt can all contain a lining.

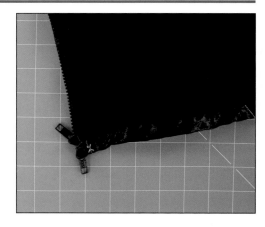

Interlining is an unseen layer of a garment that may be sand-wiched between the outer layer and the lining layer of a garment. It adds warmth but isn't used to add shaping to a garment. Interlining is commonly found in a winter coat when the outer layer and the lining do not add warmth to the garment.

Underlining is a layer of fabric that is basted to the outer layer so that the outer fabric and underlining are worked together as one layer during construction. Solid-colored underlining is commonly used under printed sheer fabric for dresses.

Interfacing is an unseen part of sewing that gives body and adds form and shaping to fabric. Interfacing is commonly used in collars, cuffs, facings (see Chapter 8), handbags and home-décor items to add shaping that the fabric alone will not provide.

Stabilizers are not seen but add stability to the fabric while you're sewing. They're commonly removed after the sewing is done. The most common uses for a stabilizer are sheer fabric and machine embroidery.

TIP

Look at Ready-Made Garments
When in doubt on how to achieve a finished result, look at clothing in your closet or in retail stores. Although those items may not be exactly what you want to make, you can use those same construction techniques to sew whatever you have in mind.

Lining not only hides seams and construction details but protects the inside details from damage and wear.

Lining is sewn as a separate item before it is sewn into the garment or project. Garments or projects may be fully or partially lined.

The fabric care instructions for the lining must match the outer fabric's care instructions.

Lining a garment can cause static cling. Watch for "anti-static" finishes on the bolt end information to prevent static buildup as you move in a garment.

TIP

Be Daring!
Lining doesn't always have to be a boring solid. Have fun and use prints that you love, but would never use for a garment, to line handbags and totes. You might even smile when you reach for your wallet to pay a bill.

Interlining

Adding interlining is the solution to using lightweight fabric and lining that offer no warmth. It provides insulation from the cold in a winter coat. You've probably worn something with interlining and never even knew it was there.

Common choices for interlining are blanket fabric, wool, felt, and fleece.

Interlining is protected during laundering because it is hidden inside, although it still needs to have the same care instructions as the outer fabric and the lining.

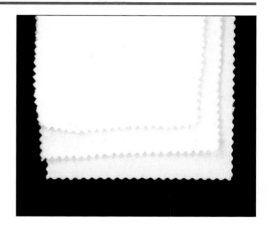

TIP

Interlining on Hand!

You may not need to buy interlining. If you have a stash of blankets that you never use, they may make perfect interlining for your project. Save the scraps for using inside potholders.

Underlining

Underlining is perfect to use with sheer fabric to make a garment and yet still maintain some modesty.

Underlining is basted to the sheer outer layer of fabric and worked as one piece of fabric.

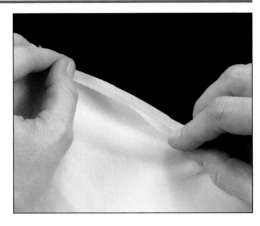

It helps keep seams and construction detail from showing through sheer fabric.

SEW-IN INTERFACING

Lightweight to medium-weight sew-in interfacing is basted to the seam line of the wrong side of the piece that will be interfaced and trimmed back to eliminate bulk in seams.

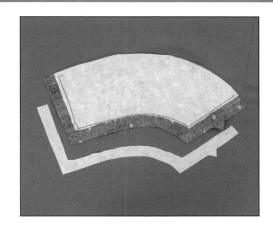

Heavyweight sew-in interfacing is sewn by removing the seam allowances, butting the seam lines to each other, and joining the pieces using a long, wide zigzag stitch to reduce bulk.

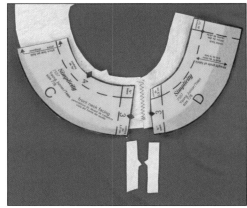

FAQ

What weight interfacing should I buy?

When in doubt, drape the interfacing with the fabric over it on your extended hand. Watch for how the combination drapes and bends. Experiment with different combinations until you have results that appeal to you.

chapter 6

Sewing Seams and Seam Finishes

Seams are the foundation of sewing. A seam holds two pieces of fabric together and should be strong and dependable. In this chapter, you'll learn all of the steps required to make sewing seams and seam finishes trouble-free.

Most sewing machines have built-in seam guides, and some machines have an additional seam guide that can be used to prevent you from sewing beyond a set limit. In addition to sewing-related seam guides, you can use simple items from an office supply store.

The presser foot and throat plate markings offer the most commonly used seam guides; these are etched into the throat plate.

Attachable seam guides, as shown, offer a barrier to prevent the seam allowance from going beyond the desired guide.

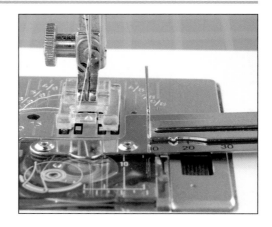

Masking tape, magnetic seam guides, and even a pad of sticky notes can be placed on the sewing machine bed as a seam guide.

Note: You can use the corner of a pad of sticky notes as a seam guide to turn corners and sew circles.

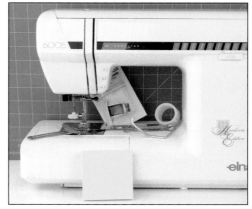

Testing a seam guide ensures that you'll be sewing the seam allowance that you want and offers you endless possibilities for setting up unusual seam guides.

① Place a tape measure horizontally under the sewing machine needle, and insert the needle into the tape measure at your desired seam allowance measurement.

② Place your desired seam guide at the end of the tape measure or verify that the machine markings are correct.

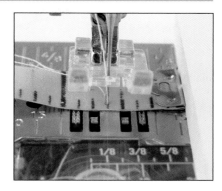

③ Turn the tape measure vertically to set a seam guide for turning a corner.

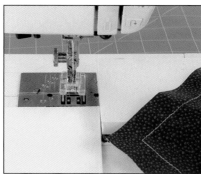

TIP

Best Way to Alter

Changing the seam allowance that is listed on a pattern can alter the way the finished item fits. Making a garment longer by using smaller seam allowances on all horizontal seams may seem like a solution, but you'll be changing where the bust line, waistline, and hip line land on the garment. Use adjustment lines marked on the pattern before you cut out the pattern instead.

When you sew a seam, straight or curved, the seam allowance needs to be even and consistent for the length of the seam. Keeping your stitches straight is the key to having a smooth seam on the outside of the garment.

① Set your seam guide. Align the fabric under the presser foot so that the seam allowance is butted to the seam guide and a few stitches' worth of fabric are behind the needle.

② Reverse stitch to the front end of the fabric, stopping so that the last stitch is at the end of the fabric.

TIP

Watch the Guide

Always watch the guide and not the needle. Watching the needle is the most common reason for wandering stitches.

③ Sew forward, keeping the edge of the seam allowance at the seam guide. Sew slowly until you gain full control of your sewing machine's speed.

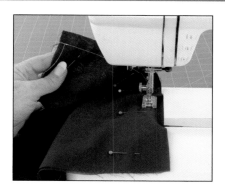

④ To end the seam, sew to the end of the fabric and then reverse-stitch three or four stitches before raising the presser foot and removing the fabric.

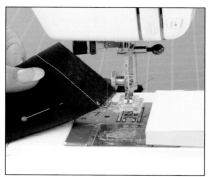

TIP

Crooked Stitching
Crooked stitching should be removed. You can remove the faulty stitching without removing the entire seam. Sew a few stitches on top of the correct stitching at each end to lock the replacement and existing stitches.

Pressing during garment construction is the difference between a professional-looking result and one that looks somewhat amateur. Pressing involves moving the iron up and down instead of pushing back and forth across the fabric, which can distort the fibers.

① The first step to pressing while you are sewing is to press as it was sewn. In the case of a seam, press the fabric exactly as it was sewn when the fabric was under the presser foot. This sets the stitches in the fabric.

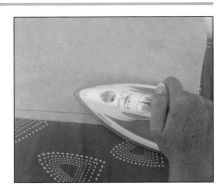

② To create a pressed open seam, open the fabric and press the seam open with the tip of the iron.

③ Press again from the right side of the fabric. Repeat until the fabric and seam lie smoothly.

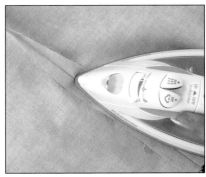

TIP

Pressing Curves

A pressing ham is a great tool to use to press curves. You can also use towels rolled and folded to get the shape you need to support a curved seam.

The only variation to sewing a curved seam is that the seam allowance curves to follow the edge of the fabric. As with any seam, the seam allowance must stay consistent.

A continuous curved seam or circle does not need to be back-stitched. When the sewing comes to the first stitches, sew over the first three or four stitches to secure the stitching in the fabric.

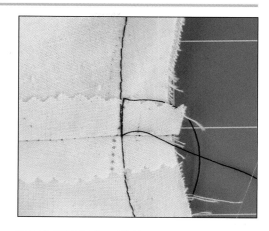

A curved seam usually requires clipping or notching for the seam to lie smoothly. It is important to not weaken the seam when you clip or notch the seam. Clip only in the seam allowance, leaving the seam line intact to preserve the seam's integrity.

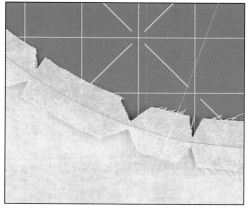

Finished seams will help fabric that is prone to fraying remain strong and stable. Use scraps of your fabric to experiment with the type of seam finish that will work best with your fabric.

Tightly woven fabric that is not prone to fraying but could fray after laundering can be finished by using pinking shears on the edge of the seam allowance.

Combining straight stitching just inside the pinked edge offers one more step to reinforcing a seam allowance.

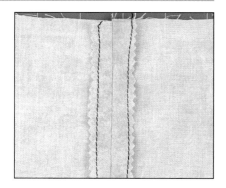

If it won't create bulk that will show though to the outside of the fabric, a seam allowance can also be finished by pressing under ⅛ inch of the seam allowance and stitching the turned edge with a straight stitch.

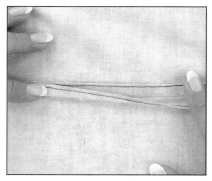

FAQ

How do I finish a crotch seam that is trimmed down?

Crotch seams are commonly sewn with the seam and a second row of stitching just inside the seam line and then trimmed. A zigzag stitch may also be sewn on the edge to prevent fraying.

Zigzag Seam Finish

A zigzag seam finish is one of the easiest and fastest seam finishes you can sew with a sewing machine.

1. Sew and press the seam as instructed in your pattern.

2. With the seam pressed open, move all the fabric, except the seam allowance you'll be sewing, out of the way.

3. Set your sewing machine for a zigzag stitch that's wide enough to enclose approximately one-quarter of the seam allowance.

4. Place the seam allowance only under the presser foot so that the right swing of the needle encloses the edge of the seam allowance. Find a guide on the presser foot to align the edge of the seam allowance.

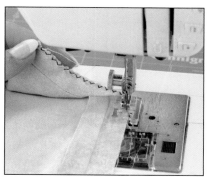

FAQ

How can I keep a zigzagged seam finish from being so bulky?

Elongate the stitch length so that the stitching is spread out. It will enclose the seam allowance, but the stitching will not be dense enough to create bulk.

Lace Inset Seam

Lace and other decorative details are often set into a seam line. Lace is available in many weights and densities. Your choice should be matched to the weight of your fabric or lighter to prevent heavy lace from adding excessive bulk to the seam.

GATHERED LACE

1. Gathered lace can be added to straight or curved seams. Position the lace on the fabric so the gathered edge or edge you want enclosed is toward the seam allowance.

2. Baste the edge in place so the edge of the lace will be in the seam allowance when you sew the seam.

3. Finish the seam as desired.

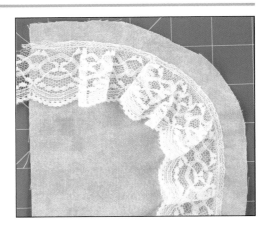

STRAIGHT LACE

1. Straight lace can only be added to straight seams. Sandwich the lace between the fabrics and sew the seam.

2. Finish the seam as desired.

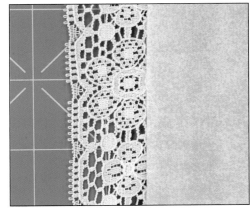

Adding cording or piping to a seam is common in home décor and garments. Piping is bulkier than fabric, so you need to use a zipper foot or cording foot on your sewing machine.

1 Using a zipper foot or cording foot, sew the piping to the right side of one layer of the fabric with the stitching at the seam line.

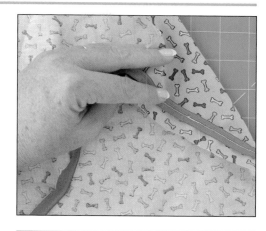

2 Enclose the piping by placing a second layer of fabric over the fabric with the piping–right sides together.

3 Stitch the two pieces of fabric, with the piping sandwiched between, on the original stitch line. Keep the stitching tight to the piping.

Note: Clip and notch corners to allow the piping to lie smoothly as shown on p. 78–79.

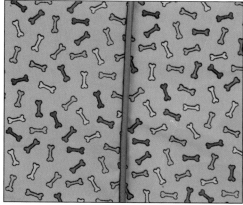

Markings (or dots) and seam guides will help you to determine when to stop sewing and prepare to turn a corner. To sew a corner: Stop with the sewing machine needle down, raise the presser foot, turn the fabric to the seam guide, and lower the presser foot to continue sewing.

SEW AN OUTSIDE CORNER WITH SEAM INSETS

Turning corners with lace, piping, or trims will require extra attention so that the inset item will turn with the angle you're sewing.

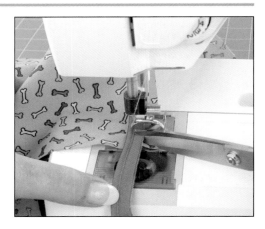

1. Sew on the trim, stopping with the needle down at the corner of the seam line.

2. Raise the presser foot and clip the seam allowance of the trim close to the stitch line.

3. Rotate the fabric and trim to line up the next side you will be sewing.

4. Lower the presser foot and continue sewing.

SEW AN INSIDE CORNER WITH SEAM INSETS

An inside corner can cause trim to turn back on itself, creating extra bulk and the possibility of sewing over the trim's seam allowance. Here is a solution:

① Sew on the trim, stopping with the needle down at the corner.

② Raise the presser foot and cut a V in the trim seam allowance.

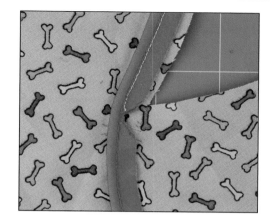

③ Pivot the fabric and trim to set up sewing the next edge closing in the V notch.

④ Lower the presser foot and continue sewing.

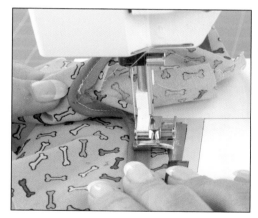

FAQ

How do I eliminate the bulkiness at the corners of my pillows?

Try trimming each corner to eliminate the bulk. Another trick is to "square-off" the corner, by turning the corner halfway and sewing two to three diagonal stitches, and then turning again to finish the rest of the corner.

Many seams require a rounded edge to be joined to a straight edge of fabric, such as a sleeve on a jacket. At first it looks as though there is no way the two edges can possibly fit together. Easing in the rounded edge, without creating any tucks or gathers, is possible when you know how to ease in the fabric.

1 Sew two or three lines of machine basting stitches on the rounded piece of fabric in the seam allowance, close to the seam line, leaving a thread tail at the end of your stitching.

2 Pin the round-edged fabric to the straight-edged fabric, matching any pattern markings.

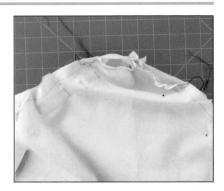

3 Pull the ends of the basting thread to bring the fibers of the fabric closer to each other and to fit the rounded edge to the straight edge of the fabric. Pin in place and be sure the seam line of the rounded-edge fabric is smooth, and the fullness is evenly distributed, before machine sewing it in place.

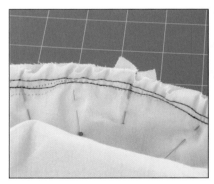

TIP

Machine Basting Next to a Seam Line
Changing needle position is a great way to control where your lines of machine basting will be sewn. Set your fabric to a seam guide for the seam allowance of the finished seam, and change the needle position one to three positions to the right of the seam line.

Gathers, commonly used in home décor and garment sewing, should not have any tucks or folds. For a professional appearance, evenly distribute the gathers.

1 Sew two or three lines of machine basting stitches on the seam allowance just inside the seam line of the fabric that will be gathered. You'll need to leave a thread tail at the end of the basting stitches.

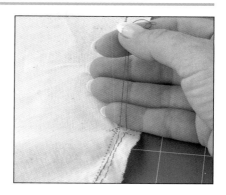

2 Pin the fabric that will be gathered to the flat fabric, matching any pattern markings.

3 Pull the threads at the end of the basting to gather the fabric. Evenly distribute the fullness and stitch the seam.

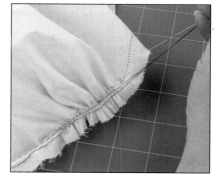

TIP

Gathering Heavy Fabric

Heavy fabric can be difficult to gather with basting threads. Zigzag over a piece of string, on the seam allowance, without stitching on the string. To gather the fabric, pull the string while being careful not to pull the other end of the string through.

chapter 7

Shaping Details

Straight seams and straight fabric are great for a simple tote bag or a pillowcase, but bodies have curves. Taking a straight piece of fabric and transforming it to fit those curves requires shaping details such as darts, pleats, and curved seams. Waistbands and elastic contribute to shaping a garment. Properly sewing those elements contributes to how the garment will drape on a body.

Dart Markings

Darts are a sewing element, which are gradual tucks of fabric sewn into a point. The point of a dart should be "angled" gradually so that the end will lie smoothly and blend into the fibers of the fabric.

Dart markings must be transferred from the pattern to the wrong side of the fabric in order for the dart to be in the correct location on the garment.

Transfer the dots and stitching lines onto the wrong side of the fabric. Connect the dots whenever possible using carbon paper and a tracing wheel as shown in the photo below or use one of the other marking methods listed on p. 25.

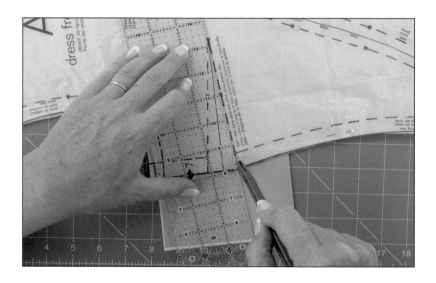

Pin and Baste Darts

Darts must be held in place as you sew them. Because sewing over straight pins is not an option, you can either remove the straight pins as you sew or baste the dart.

1 Using the dots and seam lines, match the markings on both sides of the dart by inserting a straight pin into one dot and through the matching dot on the other side of the dart. Fold the fabric, bringing the pin insertion points together, and weave the pin through the fabric to anchor the pin.

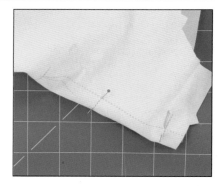

2 If you aren't comfortable removing pins as you sew, hand-baste the dart. See p. 35 for hand basting techniques.

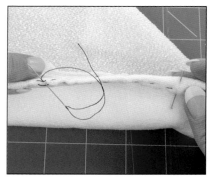

TIP

Altering Darts

Any adjustment to where a dart will appear must be made on the pattern before the pattern is cut out. "Winging it" to make a dart adjustment can distort the line of the dart and the drape of the fabric. If you're not sure of the placement, make a quick draft of the pattern in an inexpensive fabric, such as muslin, before cutting out your fabric.

Sewing Darts

Darts come in different sizes and shapes, but they're all sewn in the same basic order.

---

1 Starting at the widest part of the dart, place the sewing machine needle in the dart's seam.

2 Put the presser foot down and backstitch if the widest part of the dart is in the seam line. For a double-ended dart, start just behind the center of the dart and sew to each pointed end, overlapping your stitches in the center.

3 With a regular stitch length, sew, following the stitching line until the next-to-the-last dot on the dart.

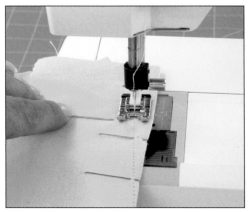

4 Gradually shorten the stitch length to the smallest possible stitch without puckering the fabric. Sew two to three stitches off the end of the dart, tapering off the end of the dart so that the last stitch may only catch one thread of the fabric.

5 Leave a thread tail as you remove the material from the sewing machine.

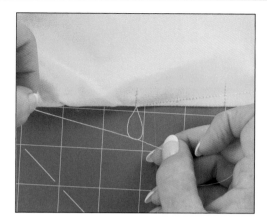

6 Make two square knots, bringing the knots to the end of the machine stitching.

7 Trim the threads close to the knots.

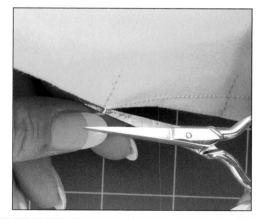

TIP

Changing Stitch Length

The length of the stitches may affect whether or not your stitching will pucker the fabric. Use scraps of fabric to test how short a stitch length you can use before the fabric will pucker. Practicing on a scrap is much better than trying to remove tiny stitches.

Many darts will require that the body of the dart be clipped so that it lies smoothly. Curved darts and double-ended darts are the most common darts to require clipping, but any dart that won't lie flat to the body of the fabric will need to be clipped.

① Clip at the dot in the area where the dart fabric will not lie against the body of the fabric.

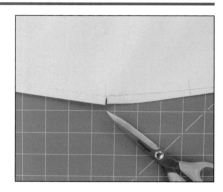

② If you're using loosely woven fabric, which is apt to fray through the center of the dart, reinforce the fabric by stitching a second row just inside the original stitching.

③ Press the darts as directed in the pattern instructions, usually down or toward the center.

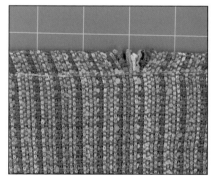

TIP

Prevent Over-Clipping

Using sharp scissors and knowing where the point of the scissors will land are critical in order to avoid clipping into the stitching line. Insert a straight pin slightly inside the seam line to prevent the scissors from clipping into the stitching.

Bulky and Wide Darts

A wide dart and a dart in thick fabric can create bulk that will push through the right side of the garment. There are ways to eliminate that bulk.

1 On a bulky fabric or wide dart made with fabric that is not prone to fraying, trim the body of the dart, leaving a seam allowance's worth of fabric, to within ½ to 1 inch from the point of the dart.

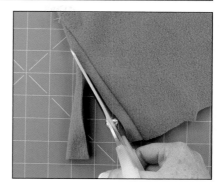

2 Press the dart as it was sewn and then as directed in the pattern instructions. If the fabric is still bulky, press the dart open, flattening the dart to the point.

TIP

No Seam Finish on Darts
Many bulky fabrics are also loosely woven. Do not attempt to add a seam finish to the trimmed dart. Stitch just inside the original stitching line on the dart if necessary to protect the trimmed dart.

Pleats are even folds of fabric that are pressed into place. Pleats are usually included in the pattern, with the amount of fabric the pleat will take built into a pattern piece. A pattern marking key will explain the markings on the pattern.

SIDE PLEATS

Side (or knife) pleats have even folds that all face in the same direction. This type of pleat has one fold line marking and one placement line marking.

① Transfer the pattern markings to the wrong side of the fabric using one of the marking methods listed in Chapter 2.

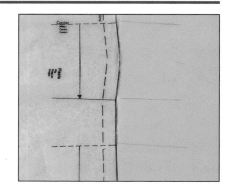

② Fold the fabric, wrong sides together, on the fold line, bringing the fold to the placement line to create a pleat. Pin and press well.

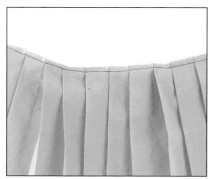

TIP

When you can't see the marking you need, rather than mark on the right side of the fabric, place straight pins at the marking, through the fabric, and use the straight pins as the markings on the right side of the fabric.

BOX PLEATS

Box pleats are made with two even folds turned away from each other, with the underside folds meeting each other.

INVERTED PLEATS

An inverted pleat is made the same way as a box pleat except that the meeting edges are on the right side of the garment.

An inverted pleat can add a decorative element by using a contrasting fabric. Simply allow seam allowances when you replace the "back" of the pleat.

Waistbands bring the garment in to fit the body. Most waistbands have an opening so that the band can be opened to get into and out of the garment.

① Transfer the pattern markings to the waistband and to the garment where the waistband will be attached.

② Interface waistbands so that they will be firm.

③ Stay-stitch (see p. 96) the body of the fabric where the waistband will be attached to prevent the fabric from distorting or stretching out of shape.

④ Follow the pattern directions to attach the waistband, using the pattern markings to align the waistband.

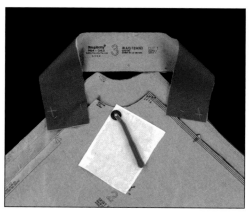

⑤ Trim the corners and grade the seams to prevent bulky lines from showing through the waistband.

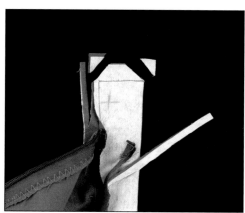

Using Elastic

Elastic is another way to make garments fit the body and stretch with movement. It also allows you to easily get into and out of the garment—not to mention that it has weight-forgiving properties. Elastic is available in a variety of weights and forms. Heavy, non-roll elastic is recommended for waistbands.

Most elastic is threaded through a casing and sewn to itself to allow the elastic to move freely inside the casing.

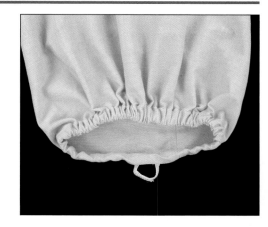

Elastic sewn directly to the fabric must be sewn with a stretch stitch and the elastic being stretched as it is sewn. A zigzag stitch is the most commonly used stretch stitch, but other options are available on higher-end sewing machines.

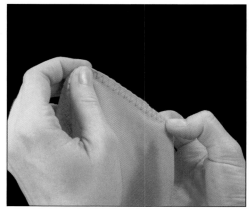

chapter 8

Edge Finishes and Facings

Edge finishing techniques are needed to enclose raw edges. A properly sewn facing will stay inside the garment and never be seen from the right side. Other edge finishes can be hidden inside or moved to the outside as a decorative detail.

A facing is a separate piece of fabric that maintains the shape and finishes of an edge. To get results you can be proud of in your end product, some preparation steps are needed on facings.

① Transfer pattern markings onto the facing and interfacing.

② Stay-stitch and interface the facing pieces before joining any facing pieces.

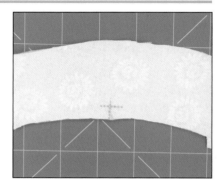

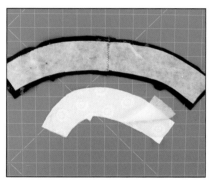

FAQ

Why should I stay-stitch?

Because stay-stitching doesn't join layers of fabric, many people think it's a waste of time. Wrong! Stay-stitching stabilizes off-grain edges of cut fabric. Stabilizing these edges is essential to prevent the edges from stretching or becoming distorted while the piece is handled or pressed. If it becomes distorted, it won't fit together with pieces that are supposed to join to it.

3 Follow the pattern directions to join the facing pieces since there are many methods to join facings, which depend on whether it is a neck, armhole, front, or other type of facing.

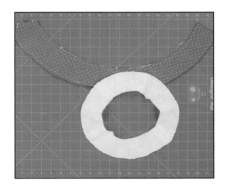

4 Finish the edge of the facing before it is joined to the garment. On cotton-weight fabrics, the fabric is usually finished by stitching ¼ inch from the raw edge, then pressing the raw edge to the wrong side of the facing along the stitching line and stitching.

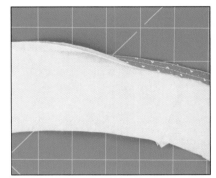

> ## TIP
>
> ### Edge Finishes on Facings
> The seam finish you use on seams can usually be used to finish the edge of a facing. Your goal is to have the edge of the facing lie smooth and not press through to the outside of the garment.

Grade Facing Seam Allowances

Very few patterns will tell you to grade a seam, but it's the best way to eliminate bulk and gain control over the facing to have it lie smoothly.

① After sewing the facing to the garment, trim the seam allowance in half.

② Trim the facing seam allowance in half again, so that it's shorter than the garment seam allowance.

FAQ

What is grading?

Grading is trimming a seam allowance so the layers of the seam allowance are at different widths. It eliminates a sharp, bulky edge that may show through to the right side of the garment.

Clip Facing
Seam Allowances

Clipping is used to help curved edges lie smoothly. Never clip the stitching or the seam will unravel.

1 Clip the seam allowance of an inside curved area by making small clips cutting into the seam allowance only without cutting any of the stitches.

2 Loosely woven fabric can be weakened by clipping. Clip one layer of the seam allowance and move over to cut the other layer in a different place to prevent weakening the seam.

TIP

Seam Stability
Many curved seams will require you to clip the seam allowance, not just facings. Keep the seam strong by using the clipping method for loosely woven fabric.

Under-stitching is sometimes called *stitch-in-the-ditch*. Under-stitching is sewn as close to the seam as possible but not on the seam. Proper under-stitching will keep the facing on the inside of the garment.

1 Press the facing seam allowance as it was sewn and then toward the facing.

2 Place the facing under the sewing machine needle right side up, with the seam allowance under the facing.

3 Using a guide on the presser foot, align the fabric so that the needle will penetrate the fabric next to the seam on the facing. Sew, keeping the stitches an even distance from the seam.

TIP

Change the Needle Position

Changing the needle position on your sewing machine allows you to choose a guide on the presser foot and then set the needle where you want it to penetrate the fabric.

Bias Tape

Bias tape is sold in the notion section of fabric stores. It is available in a wide variety of colors, sizes, and forms. Bias tape can also be made from your own fabric for many different projects.

Single-fold bias tape has both edges folded toward the center on the wrong side of the bias tape. It is commonly used to make facings and casings and as a decorative accent.

Double-fold bias tape has the raw edges pressed under as on single-fold bias tape, but then the tape is folded in nearly half. One edge is slightly wider than the other on packaged double-fold bias tape. Double-fold bias tape is used to enclose raw edges. The slightly narrower edge is sewn on top right side so that the wider edge is on the wrong side always caught in the stitching.

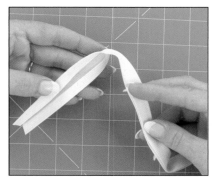

FAQ

How do I sew both edges of the double-fold bias tape on the edge of fabric when I can only see one edge?

When attaching bias tape in one step, keep the shorter side up so that the wider edge on the bottom is caught in the stitching. Hand-baste the bias tape in place to keep it from slipping.

Bias Tape Facings

Single-fold bias tape can be used as a facing on a raw edge. Many commercial patterns are now using bias tape as a facing for the edge of necklines. In these patterns, you'll only need to trim the bias-tape facing if the pattern instructs you to do so or if you're replacing a cut facing.

❶ Stay-stitch the fabric so that the fabric maintains its intended shape.

❷ Place the right side of the bias tape on the right side of the fabric, leaving a tail of bias tape on the ends to turn under or fold over the end on a continuous area. Align the fold of the bias tape on the seam line. Trim away the excess seam allowance so that the raw edges of the unfolded bias tape and fabric are even.

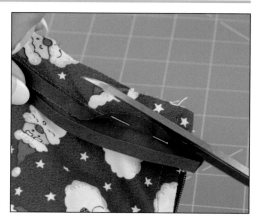

❸ Stitch the bias tape to the garment along the seam line in the fold of the bias tape as shown in the photo.

❹ Using the tip of the iron, press the new seam, so that the right sides of the fabric and bias tape are up with the seam allowance under the bias tape.

❺ Fold the bias tape up and over the seam allowance so that the right sides of both fabric and bias tape are up with the seam allowance under the bias tape. Press seam with the tip of an iron.

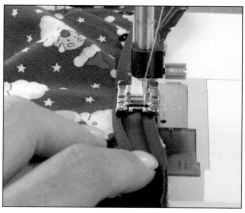

⑤ **Optional:** Under-stitch the seam allowance to the bias tape to ensure that the bias tape will stay to the inside.

⑥ Bring the wrong side of the bias tape to the wrong side of the fabric. Turn under the end tails of the bias tape at an angle so they won't show on the outside of the garment.

⑦ Press in place.

⑧ Slip-stitch or topstitch the unsewn edge of the bias tape into place.

This photo shows a finished bias tape facing.

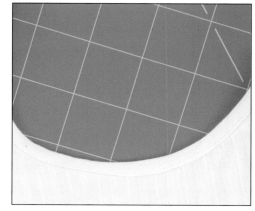

FAQ

Using bias tape as a facing is so much easier than preparing a facing. Why can't I always use bias tape as a facing?

Bias tape as a facing works very well on fabric that is the same weight as, or lighter than, the bias tape. It will not give you as structured an edge as a facing will.

Enclose an Edging with Bias Tape

Adding bias tape is a quick way to enclose raw edges on sewing projects. Try using bias tape in a contrasting or complementary color.

① If you're altering a pattern to allow an edge to be enclosed in bias tape, you must trim the edge to the seam line.

② Open the center fold of the double-fold bias tape, and place it over the raw edge.

③ Align the fold line with the true seam line of the fabric, keeping the narrower side of the bias tape on the right side of the fabric and the wider side of tape on the wrong side of the fabric.

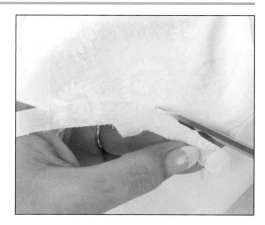

④ Leaving a ¼ to ½ inch tail of bias tape to enclose the end, start at a seam, such as an underarm seam. Pin the bias tape in place over the raw edge.

⑤ It's a good idea to hand-baste the bias tape in place so that the center fold of the bias tape stays aligned with the seam line of the fabric.

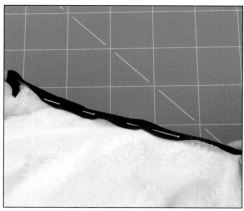

6 When the seam is in the round, such as an armhole, fold the end of the bias tape under to overlap and enclose the raw end of the bias tape.

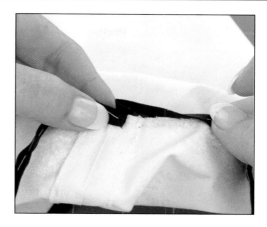

When the seam has an ending area, such as a neckline, cut the tape at the end of the fabric at an angle to eliminate bulk. Fold in the ends of the bias tape to make it even with the end of the fabric. Slipstitch the end of the bias tape closed as shown in the photo on the right.

7 Stitch bias tape to the project by topstitching the outer edge of the bias tape from the right side.

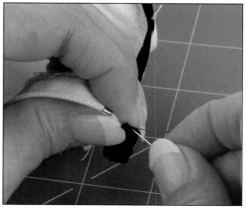

Bias tape is a versatile edge. Many times there will be corners to turn, such as a V-neck. Your goal is to make the turn as smooth and inconspicuous as possible.

1 Pin and/or hand or machine baste the bias tape until you reach the corner.

2 Fold the bias tape back on itself and down again to form a small tuck in the folded edge to make a smooth corner or turn.

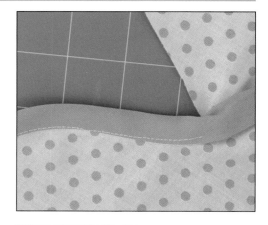

3 Topstitch the bias tape in place, stopping at the turn with the needle down. Raise the presser foot and pivot the fabric to continue sewing the bias tape. Lower the presser foot and continue sewing.

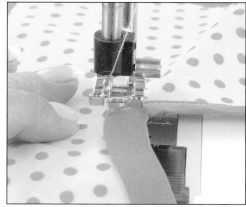

Make Your Own Bias Tape

When you create your own bias tape, you can have bias tape that perfectly matches the fabric in your sewing project.

1 Using a single layer of fabric, cut several 1-inch strips of fabric on the bias grain. Use the 45-degree angle on a rotary ruler aligned with a straight grain edge to obtain perfect bias.

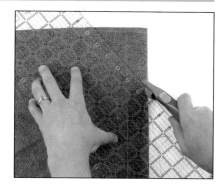

2 Use a bias tape folder with an iron to perfectly fold the bias tape as shown in the photo.

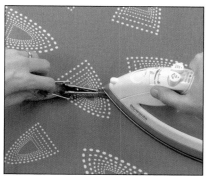

TIP

Add Your Artistic Flair

A plain blouse can be transformed into a perfect match by adding bias tape trim made from the scraps of the skirt or pants fabric. You can also make bias tape in colors and prints that are not available commercially.

chapter 9

Zippers

Installing a zipper in a garment may seem complicated, but using the information in this chapter can make the process easily manageable. You can also use these instructions for adding a zipper in home-décor items. Experiment on scraps and pillows to become more comfortable with zippers.

Before the invention of zippers, everything was buttoned. Zippers added a secure closing that we depend on everyday. In order to understand the different types of zippers and how they're installed, you need to know the parts of a zipper.

The **teeth** (1) of zippers lock together to hold the zipper closed. Zipper teeth can be polyester coils, molded polyester, or metal.

The zipper teeth are attached to a fabric **tape** (2), which provides fabric to sew the zipper onto an item. The woven nature of the zipper tape provides a stitching guideline.

The **slider** (3) has grooves that work the teeth of the zipper to open and close the teeth.

The size of the zipper **pull** (4) corresponds with the size of the zipper teeth. Decorative zipper pulls and large zipper pulls can aid someone who has difficulty grasping a small item.

Stops (5) prevent the slide from moving beyond the zipper teeth. Separating zippers have a **retaining box** (6) to bring the two sides of the zipper together and stop the slide from going beyond the bottom of the zipper.

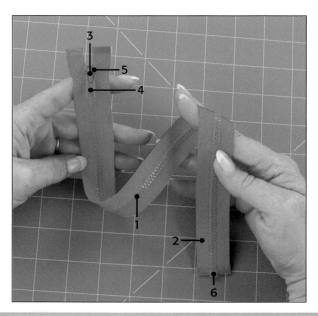

There are different types of zippers available to use for many different applications. A separating zipper separates completely, while a nonseparating zipper does not separate at the bottom. Using the correct type of zipper increases its lifespan.

All-purpose zippers (1) are the most commonly used zipper. They have polyester coils or metal teeth and are available in a variety of lengths and colors. They will separate.

Jacket zippers (2) are separating zippers and are available in a variety of weights.

Jeans zippers (3) have strong teeth and are nonseparating. The slide is low-profile with a durable lock that will lie flat under fabric.

Invisible zippers (4) are constructed of lightweight polyester coils. Their design allows the coils to hide in the seam. They require special presser feet for installation.

Specialty zippers (5) are for upholstery, sleeping bags, coveralls, and other items that require special closures. These zippers may be ordered through most fabric stores or purchased online.

Note: *A zipper made with polyester teeth will not weigh as much as a zipper made with metal teeth. The weight of the zipper can affect the way a garment will hang or stretch out of shape.*

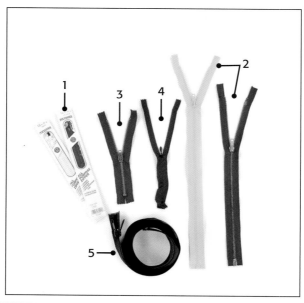

A centered zipper application has the zipper teeth directly under the center of the seam and evenly placed stitching on both sides of the zipper. It is commonly used in the center front or back of a garment.

1 Sew a normal seam with a normal stitch length until you reach the mark for the bottom of zipper. Backstitch at the mark and change sewing machine to a long basting stitch length for the area the zipper will be sewn in.

2 Apply a seam finish before sewing in a zipper.

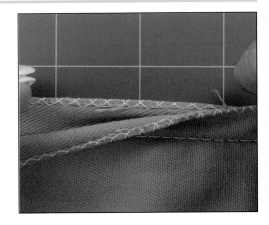

3 Press the seam as it was sewn. Using the tip of the iron to reach inside the seam, press the seam open. Then press the seam open from the right side of the fabric as well.

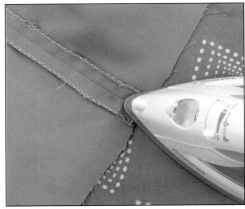

4. Open the zipper. With the pull side of the zipper on the seam, align the top of the zipper tape with the top of the seam with the right side of the zipper tape on the right side of the seam allowance.

5. Hand-baste the zipper tape to the seam allowance, keeping the edge of the zipper teeth aligned with the seam-line stitching. Baste until you reach the end of the zipper.

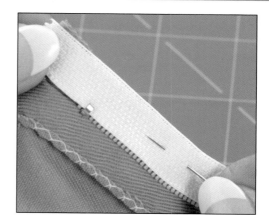

6. Close the zipper and place the zipper pull up toward the top end of the seam.

7. Hand-baste the other side of the zipper to the other seam allowance, keeping the zipper flat and smooth to the fabric.

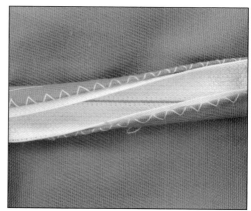

TIP

Press As You Sew

Take the time to press after each step. Pressing gives you sharp edges on your seams for the zipper teeth to follow, aiding placement of the zipper.

CONTINUED ON NEXT PAGE

8 Place the fabric under the zipper foot with the right side down on the sewing machine.

9 Set the needle to penetrate the stitching guide in the weave of the zipper tape.

10 Using a normal stitch length, sew from the top of the zipper to the bottom. Stop with the needle down at the bottom of the zipper.

11 Raise the zipper foot and pivot to sew across the bottom of the zipper to the guide on the opposite zipper tape.

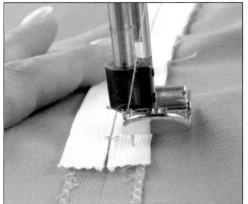

⑫ Pivot again at the stitching guide on the zipper and sew the second side of the zipper.

⑬ Backstitch at the top of the zipper.

⑭ Check that the stitching on the right side is an even distance on both sides of the seam. Remove the stitching and redo if necessary.

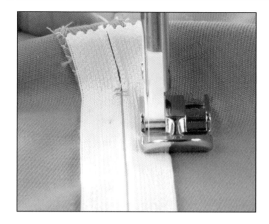

⑮ When you're satisfied with the stitching, remove the hand basting and the machine basting that are holding the seam closed.

A lapped zipper has one line of stitching showing on the outside of the garment with a "lap" of fabric concealing the zipper. This method is commonly used on side zippers or as a type of fly-front zipper on pants.

1 Using a normal stitch length, sew a normal seam until you reach the mark for the bottom of your zipper. Backstitch at the mark and change the machine to a long basting stitch. Sew the rest of the seam closed with a basting stitch.

2 Press the seam open as it was sewn. Apply a seam finish.

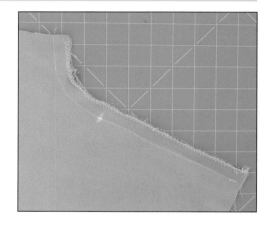

3 Place the body of the fabric to one side, leaving the right seam allowance as a single layer.

4 With the zipper closed, place the zipper, pull side down, on one side of the seam allowance, aligning the bottom of the zipper with the bottom marking and the left side of the teeth to the seam line.

5 Use a zipper foot and sew the zipper tape to the seam allowance only.

6 Fold the sewn edge under so the pull side of the zipper is facing up. Press the seam that is attached to the zipper tape to the seam allowance.

7 Stitch the pressed edge of the fabric to the zipper tape, using the opposite side of the zipper foot, close to the fold.

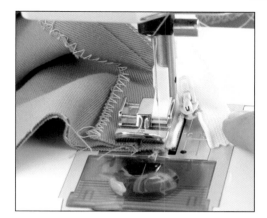

FAQ

How can I create curved stitching at the bottom of a lapped zipper?

Before you start to sew the second side of the zipper, use a round item (such as a coin or small glass) to mark a temporary curving line from the seam line at the bottom of the zipper to the guideline on the unsewn side of the zipper. Follow that line to sew the bottom of the zipper, tapering into the guideline on the zipper tape.

CONTINUED ON NEXT PAGE

8 Spread the garment out flat with the seam open. Bring the zipper over the seam allowance to form a small pleat in the seam allowance.

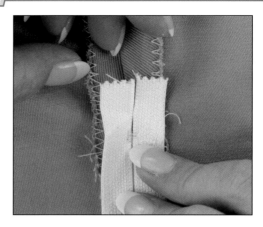

9 Starting at the bottom of the zipper, at the seam line, stitch the zipper across the end of the zipper tapes and the pleat. Stop at the guide line in the unsewn zipper tape and pivot to sew second side of the zipper through the seam allowance and garment.

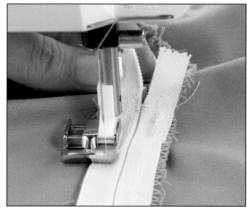

TIP

Interface the Seam Allowance

When you're working with soft, lightweight, or flimsy fabric, achieving a sharp zipper can be difficult. Lightweight interfacing applied to the seam allowance in the zipper location will overcome a limp edge on your zipper.

10 Sew the zipper to the top of the zipper.

11 Remove the basting and press.

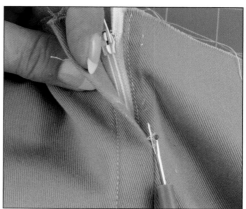

An invisible zipper is unobtrusive and does not show any construction stitches on the outside of the garment. Unlike other zippers, an invisible zipper is sewn in before any other part of the seam is sewn.

A special foot is needed to sew in an invisible zipper. These feet are sold where invisible zippers are sold. You must use the brand of foot that matches the brand of zipper so that the coil fits the foot and is held in place.

Note: *Do not sew any part of the seam to which an invisible zipper will be added.*

① Open the zipper. Set an iron on a synthetic setting so that you don't melt the zipper coil. With the zipper laying pull side down, use the tip of the iron to "uncurl" the coil and flatten the zipper tape.

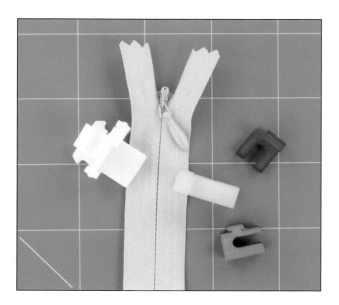

2 Place the zipper, pull side down, on the right side of the fabric, aligning the top of the zipper ¾ inch down from the top of the fabric so the coil lands on the desired seam line.

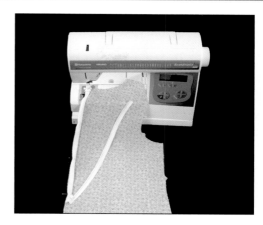

3 Place the foot of your machine so the coil is in the groove of the foot and stitch the first side.

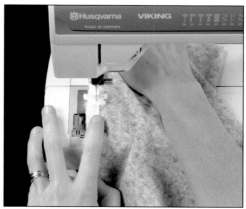

CONTINUED ON NEXT PAGE

④ Repeat for the second side of the zipper using the other side of the foot.

⑤ Close the zipper. Pin the remaining seam allowance.

⑥ Slide the zipper foot so that the needle goes through the outer notch.

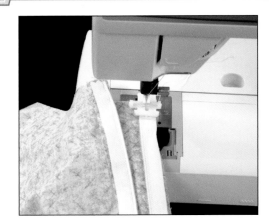

⑦ Pull the end of the zipper tape out of the way. Lower the needle just slightly above the end of the zipper stitching and approximately ⅛ inch to the left at the bottom of the zipper stitching.

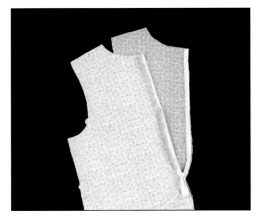

8 Lower the zipper foot and sew about 2 inches. Pull the thread to one side of the fabric and knot the threads.

9 Change to a regular presser foot and finish sewing the seam.

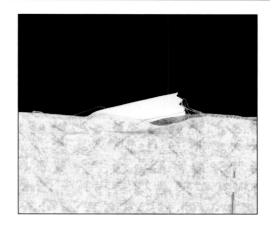

10 Apply a seam finish to the seam allowance. The photo on the right shows the completed invisible zipper side of the garment.

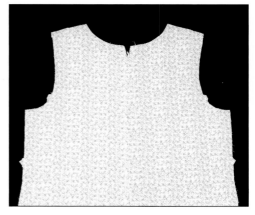

Zippers are not always available in the exact length you need. You can't lengthen a zipper, but you can shorten a zipper.

NONSEPARATING ZIPPER

1 A nonseparating zipper's length is adjusted at the bottom of the zipper. Measure the zipper and mark the zipper at the desired length.

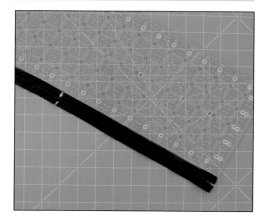

2 Use your sewing machine to sew a bar tack at the marked length.

3 Trim the end of the zipper, leaving enough tape at the bottom for installing the zipper.

4 Remove the teeth below the bar tack if possible. If the teeth can't be removed, trim them off.

5 Sew a zigzag stitch over the remaining tape below the bar tack to stabilize the tape.

SEPARATING ZIPPER

1. A separating zipper is shortened from the top of the zipper so that the retaining box at the bottom of the zipper is left intact.

2. Measuring from the bottom of the zipper, mark the zipper at the desired length.

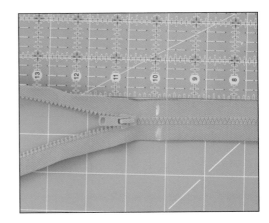

3. Move the pull back down the zipper below the mark and trim off the top of the zipper, leaving approximately 1 inch beyond the mark.

4. Sew the zipper in as you normally would.

5. Fold the top of the zipper tape over to prevent the slide from being able to slide off the teeth.

6. Trim any excess tape if needed.

chapter 10

Fasteners

A strong and reliable fastener is an integral part of keeping a garment closed. Some fasteners are almost invisible, while others add a decorative element to a garment or home-décor item.

The weight of the fabric and the dependability of the closure both play a part in the weight and size of the closure you will use. Most fasteners need to be sewn on by hand, but some can be sewn on with a sewing machine that has special feet and settings. Sewing fasteners properly contributes to how a garment will drape on a body.

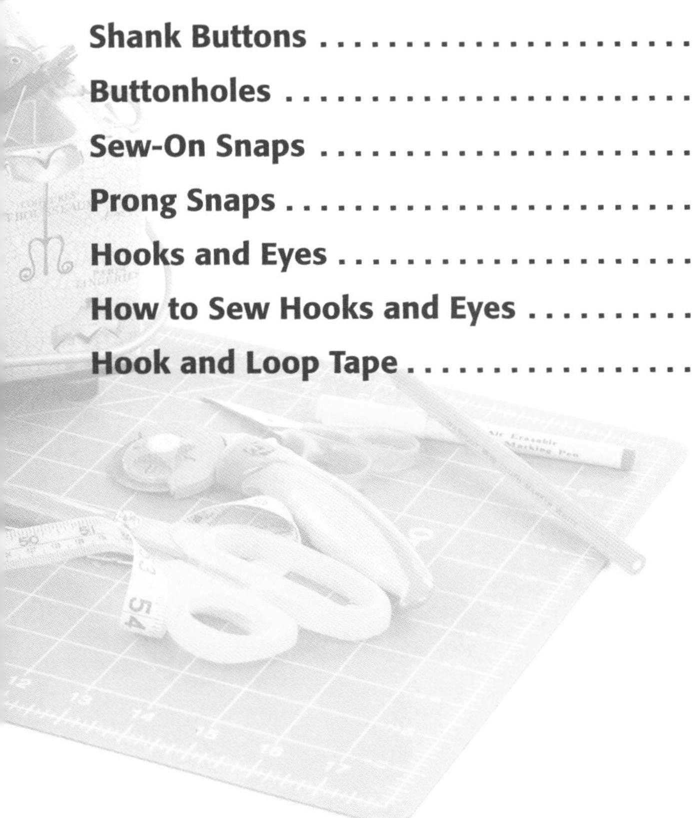

Flat buttons are the most frequently used buttons. The variety of flat buttons that are available allows them to be a subtle or decorative addition. Many sewing machines are capable of attaching flat buttons to fabric. Refer to your sewing machine manual for instructions.

Note: *You will need a spacer, such as a toothpick or straight pin, to assist with attaching a flat button.*

① Thread a hand-sewing needle with strong double thread to match the garment or the button, and knot both ends.

② Mark the placement of the button to be directly behind the buttonhole when the item is closed.

③ Sew an anchor stitch in the fabric where the button will be sewn.

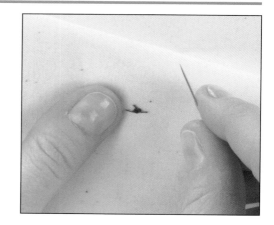

④ Bring the needle up through the button from the bottom side of the button to the top of the button.

⑤ Place the needle downward into the hole next to where the needle came up. Place a toothpick, pin, or needle on top of the button. The thread will cover the spacer to allow for the space the buttonhole fabric will take up.

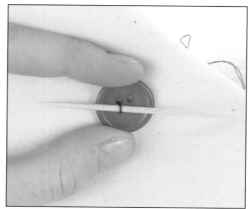

6. If you're sewing a four-hole button, bring the needle up in the empty hole next to where your needle went down in the fabric and down through the last empty hole.

7. Repeat six times for each set of holes. On the last stitch, bring the needle through the button to between the button and fabric.

8. Remove the spacer without tightening the thread. Pull the button so the threads lie smoothly on the top of the button and the excess thread is between the button and the fabric.

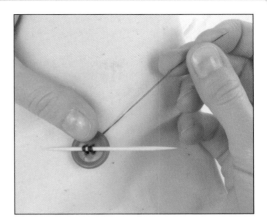

9. Wind the thread firmly around the shank of thread that is under the button.

10. Backstitch into the thread shank to secure the thread. Cut the thread close to the backstitch.

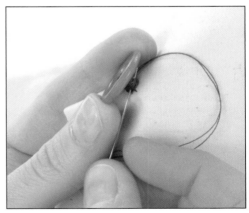

TIP

What size spacer should I use?

The thickness of the buttonhole layer of fabric is the key to how "fat" a toothpick or needle you'll use across the top of the button. A thick wool coat will require a fatter spacer than a thin silky blouse.

Shank buttons have a protruding wire or plastic section on the bottom side. They are very well suited for thick fabric. However, on lightweight fabric, the weight of a shank button tends to make the button sag rather than lie flat. Try using a shank button with a very small shank on lightweight fabric.

1 Mark the button placement as described on p. 128. The shank of the button must run the same direction as the buttonhole.

2 Anchor the thread between the facing and fabric, if possible. If there is no facing, anchor the thread on the back side of the fabric.

3 Determine how you will attach the shank to the fabric. If you are sewing a shank button to thin fabric, use very tiny stitches, keeping the button tight to the fabric.

If you're sewing a shank button to thick fabric (as shown in the photo on the right), sew through the fabric and around the shank of the button while holding the button up from the fabric. If the fabric is thicker than the shank is deep, use a spacer as described in sewing on a flat button (see p. 128).

4. Sew six to eight threads over the shank of the button.

5. Bring the needle up from the fabric without going through the shank and wrap the thread around the other threads to hold the button securely. Knot and clip the thread.

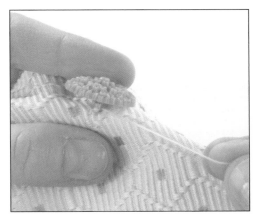

TIP

Stabilize a Shank Button on Loosely Woven or Delicate Fabric

On loosely woven or delicate fabric, sew a small flat button to the back side of the fabric to anchor the button. As the needle and thread come through to the back of the shank button, simply sew the small flat button on the back of the fabric behind the shank button.

Buttonholes can be sewn into different shapes and sizes. If your sewing machine has a buttonhole function, refer to its manual. Many electronic machines will automatically sew an entire buttonhole in one step. A loop of fabric or thread chain can act as a buttonhole to securely hold a button.

Basic buttonholes have a bar tack on each end and zigzag stitches on each side of the buttonhole. This is the most commonly used buttonhole and is perfect for almost any woven fabric.

A **stretch buttonhole** will allow the stitches to stretch with the fabric. The machine will automatically adjust, or you can lengthen the stitch length for a stretch buttonhole. The buttonhole must still be sewn to the button size to prevent the fabric from becoming distorted.

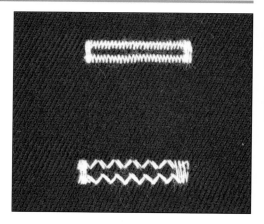

Keyhole buttonholes have a wide section, which is perfect for a button with a large shank as it allows an area for the shank while the rest of the buttonhole will lie closed.

Patterns are printed with markings for buttonhole placement. The placement lines are set for the size button that is listed on the pattern envelope.

MISSES' SHIRT: Loose fitting, button front shirt has dropped shoulders, shirt-tail hem, neckband and optional pointed collar. A and C are tunic length. B and D are below waist length. A and B have long sleeves pleated to buttoned cuffs. C and D have short sleeves.

Fabrics: Cotton and Cotton Blends such as Flannel, Gingham, Laundered Cottons, Broadcloth, Chambray, Damask, Lightweight Denim, Sateen, Seersucker. Silks and Silk Types such as Challis, Crepe, Crepe De Chine, Laundered Silks-Rayons, Lightweight Faille. Not suitable for obvious diagonals. Extra fabric needed to match plaids, stripes or one-way design fabrics. For pile, shaded or one-way design fabrics, use with nap yardages/layouts.

Notions: Thread, ¼" molded shoulder pads (opt.). **A:** Nine ½" buttons. **B:** Eight ½" buttons. **C:** Seven ½" buttons. **D:** Six ½" buttons. Look for Simplicity notions.

BODY MEASUREMENTS										
Bust	30½	31½	32½	34	36	38	40	42	44	In
Waist	23	24	25	26½	28	30	32	34	37	"
Hip-9" below waist	32½	33½	34½	36	38	40	42	44	46	"
Back-neck to waist	15½	15¾	16	16¼	16½	16¾	17	17¼	17⅜	"
Sizes	6	8	10	12	14	16	18	20	22	
Sizes-European	32	34	36	38	40	42	44	46	48	

The length of a buttonhole should equal the length of the button plus the thickness of the button. Always test your buttonholes on a scrap of the same fabric as your project before sewing them on your project.

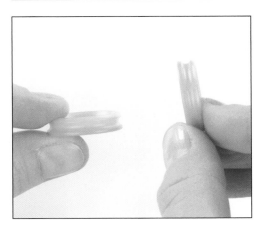

FAQ

My buttonholes are puckered. How can I avoid this?

Use a layer or multiple layers of stabilizer to stop the fabric from puckering. Test using layers of stabilizer and removing the stabilizer on scraps of fabric before sewing buttonholes on your garment.

Snaps are an inconspicuous way to close an opening. Snaps are available in a variety of sizes and weights to fit almost any need. Just as you choose buttons, the size of the snap will correspond with the weight of the fabric. A very fine fabric will use a smaller, lighter snap than a heavy fabric.

1 Thread a hand-sewing needle with a double thread and knot both threads. Anchor the knot between layers of fabric or on the wrong side of the fabric, directly under the location of the snap.

2 Place the ball half of the snap in place, bringing the thread to the outside edge of one of the holes in the snap.

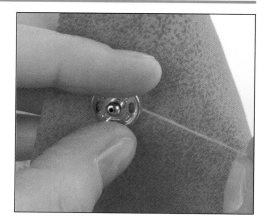

3 Push the needle through the sewing hole in the snap, penetrating just one layer of fabric if you don't want the thread to show on the outside of the item.

4 Bring the needle up next to where you placed the thread at the edge of the snap. Continue stitching to cover the whole area.

5 Bring the needle up at the next sewing hole and repeat until all the holes are attached. Knot the thread on the underside of the snap.

6 Coat the ball of the snap with tailor's chalk.

7 Bring the fabric that will be holding the other side of the snap over on top of the ball half of the snap correctly aligning the closure. Press down on the ball of the snap to mark where the second half of the snap will need to be placed.

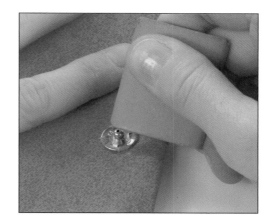

8 Use the chalk marking to place the other side of the snap by placing the center of the other half over the marking with the ball side toward the garment.

9 Sew the second side of the snap the same way you sewed the ball half of the snap.

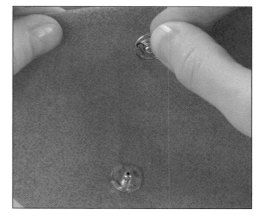

TIP

Fake Buttons

Sew a button on the outside of the fabric over a snap to give the illusion of buttons and buttonholes without the frustration of sewing buttonholes on delicate fabric.

Prong snaps provide a strong and visible closure. They are available in many different colors, finishes, and sizes, which makes them decorative as well as functional closures.

Note: *All prong snaps require some kind of tool to attach them to fabric.*

Once placed, removing a pronged snap is difficult and will leave visible damage to the fabric. Test to check that the prongs are long enough for the thickness of your fabric and to prevent damage from snaps being pulled out of the fabric when in use.

Always test the reliability of the tool and snap on scraps of the same fabric as your project to ensure that they will stay attached to the fabric and seat correctly.

Backing fabric with interfacing where a prong snap will be placed increases the stability and strength of the fabric.

Pronged snaps can be used without their counterpart to add a decorative flair and make the functioning snap blend into the design.

FAQ

Where can I find decorative snaps that are similar to those I've see on ready-made clothing?

A well-stocked local fabric store will carry a variety of snaps. Many sources are available on the Internet through companies that specialize in prong snaps.

Hooks and eyes are used as fasteners to close areas such as waistbands and necklines. They can reinforce a closure, such as the top of a zipper, or act as a stand-alone closure for a waistband.

They are sold in sets, but it is not necessary to use both parts of the set as a thread eye can be made as shown (a).

Straight hooks (b) allow the hook to sit tight to the fabric, for example, on an overlapping waistband.

Rounded hooks (c) can flex while closing two edges of fabric together, such as the top of a zipper at a neckline.

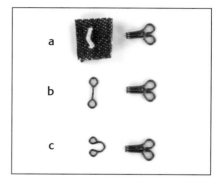

A strong flat hook and eye is designed for the hook to easily slide on and off the eye. They're strong enough for a waistband closure that may experience a strong pulling effect.

TIP

Heavy, flat hook and eye sets are sewn in the same manner without the anchor at the hook.

A hook and eye fastener is attached by hand-sewing. Sewing them properly will ensure that the hook and eye will hold the fabric closed flat as you intended. They are always sewn to the inside of a garment and not meant to be seen.

Note: *On a lapped waistband-type closure, the hook is always sewn on the inside of the outer layer of an overlapping garment.*

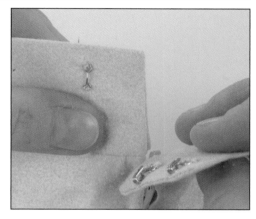

1 Anchor the thread and sew on the two loop ends of the hook in the same manner that you sew on a snap (see p. 134). Anchor the hook, sewing under the hook area.

CONTINUED ON NEXT PAGE

2 Lay the garment closed. With a straight pin, mark the location where the hook will lie in the eye.

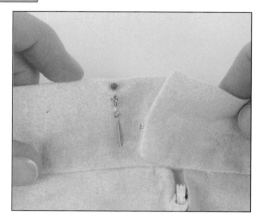

3 Sew the eye in the marked location, by sewing the loops of the eye to the fabric.

4 Place the eye on the hook and overlap the garment.

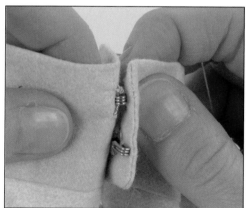

TIP

How to Determine the Size of a Hook and Eye

It depends on the weight of the fabric and the amount of pull that the hook and eye will endure. Anyone who has tried to wear a tight pair of jeans will testify to the strong pulling the waistband will endure, compared to the amount of pull at the top of a faced neckline.

Note: *Faced edges such as a neckline or facing waistband will require a rounded eye. Use one when there is any type of gap at the top of a zipper.*

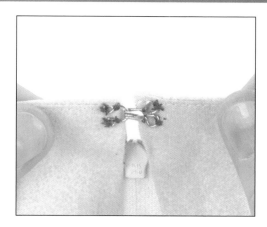

5 Use a thread eye when you want to eliminate a metal eye. Mark where the eye will intersect the hook, noting the width of the hook.

6 Anchor the thread at one end and sew three loose loops of thread the width of the hook. Sew a blanket stitch over the thread loops. Anchor and cut the thread. See p. 42 for the blanket stitch.

Looking closely at the tape, one side is formed with tiny hooks while the other side that adheres to the hooks is made up of loops.

Hook and loop tape is available in various sizes, weights, and colors. Precut hook and loop tape allows for quick closures without having to cut them yourself. Hook and loop tape is available in sew-on and adhesive-back forms.

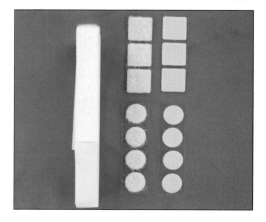

Rectangles and squares of hook and loop tape are sewn on the edges of the shape by pivoting, with the needle down, at the corners.

Always plan hook and loop tape closures before you sew the item, so that stitching lines are on an underlayer of fabric and will not be seen on the outside of a finished item as shown in the photo on the right.

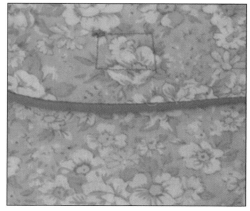

Circles of hook and loop tape are sewn on by sewing an X through the circle, backstitching at the beginning and end of your stitching for a secure hold.

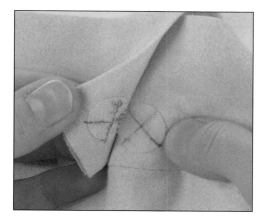

Adhesive-back hook and loop tape will gum up your sewing machine needle and the adhesive can bleed through fabric. It is best to use adhesive-back only when it cannot be sewn.

TIP

Hook and loop closures can be used instead of zippers as a fast way to close openings in Halloween costumes, pillows, slipcovers, and so on.

chapter 11

Hemming Techniques

Hemlines change with the times, but you don't have to discard pants or skirts that you love when fashion trends change. In this chapter, you'll learn how to prepare and sew a hem as well as lengthen a hem even when you thought there wasn't enough fabric on the original hem.

A hem adds weight to the bottom of a curtain or garment, which affects the way it will hang. The fabric and the design of the garment will play a role in the amount of hem you'll use.

The goal in choosing the amount of hem on a garment is to leave enough so that the item will hang properly. When in doubt, look to similar ready-made garments as a rule of thumb.

A straight, slightly flared, or gathered garment will hold a 1½- to 3-inch hem. The lighter the fabric, the more likely you are to use 3 inches to obtain more weight in the hem; the heavier the fabric, the more likely you are to use 1½ to 2 inches to eliminate bulk.

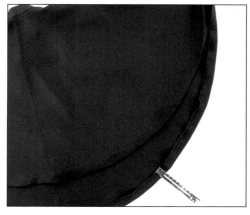

A hem on a circular skirt as shown in the photo on the right will be a 1-inch hem for most fabrics. The circular style of the garment will require the hem to be eased in order for the hem to lie smoothly.

A hem is usually finished with the same type of seam finish that is sewn throughout the garment. When replacing a hem, look carefully at the original hem before you remove it.

Sew hem tape or lace to the edge of heavy fabric to eliminate the bulk that would show through to the right side if the fabric were turned under.

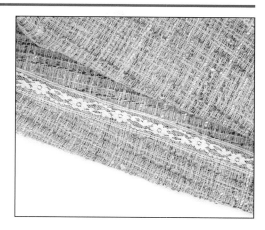

A faced hem, using bias tape or bias-cut fabric, is the perfect solution to a full or curved hem.

Fabric turned under the same length as the hem can be used to add rigidity and weight to the hem.

Mark a Garment Hem

A hem should hang an even distance from the floor at all points around the hem.

① If you are changing the hem of an existing garment, prepare the garment by removing the original hem and pressing it.

② Try on the garment with the same type of undergarments and shoes that you would wear with the garment.

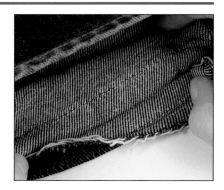

③ Mark the desired hem length using a hem marking tool or by having a friend measure the distance from the floor to the desired hem.

④ Lay the garment on a flat surface and mark the hem evenly on the entire edge that will be hemmed.

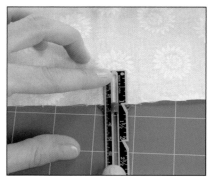

TIP

A Bias Skirt

A skirt that is made with fabric that has been cut on the bias must be hung for at least 24 hours before you attempt to hem it. This gives the fibers time to relax and hang in their new position so that you can achieve a straight hem.

Turn and Prepare the Hem

After marking the hem, you must prepare the hem edge. Your goal is to have no folds, lumps, or bumps—just a smooth continuous edge.

1 Mark the desired finished length with straight pins for easy removal or tailor's chalk for a temporary marking.

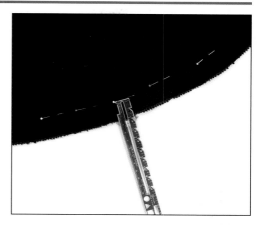

2 Turn the hem up, to the inside of the garment, at the markings all the way around the garment and press.

3 Try on the garment to be sure you are happy with the length.

4 Press the bottom fold of the hem.

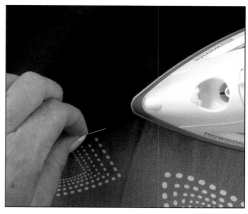

CONTINUED ON NEXT PAGE

⑤ With the hem on a flat surface, mark the desired amount of hem, measuring from the pressed edge with a gauge.

⑥ Carefully trim away any excess hem fabric, allowing for any fabric that may be needed for a seam finish.

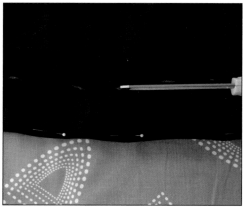

TIP

Holding the Hem in Place
A hand-sewn running stitch (basting) just above the fold line will help hold the hem in place as you finish the hem.

7 Apply a seam finish to the raw edge of the fabric. On heavy fabric, apply seam binding.

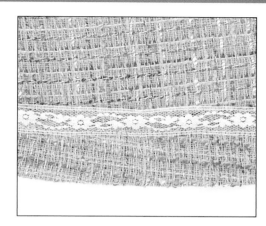

8 **Optional:** Ease in any fullness in the hem by using a row or two of machine basting at the seam-finished edge of the hem pulling up the threads until the hem lays flat.

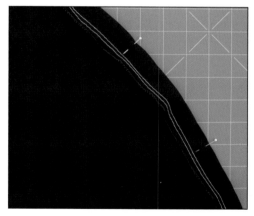

TIP

Keep It Tuck-Free!

It may seem quick and easy to just tuck in excess fullness on a hemline, but those folds of fabric will eventually show through to the outside as bulk.

A topstitched hem has a line or two of machine stitching on the outside of the garment. Accurate measurements and seam guides make straight topstitching possible.

---

1 Measure the width of hem that has been turned up, and be sure it is perfectly even for the entire hem and press fold.

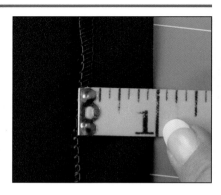

2 Set a seam guide a little less than the amount of hem.

3 Place the hem, right side up, under the needle and align the folded edge of the hem with the seam guide. Put the needle down and be sure it is penetrating the hem.

TIP

Even Double Rows of Topstitching!
Use a double or triple needle to create perfectly spaced rows of topstitching. Test the stitching on a replicated scrap of hem before you sew the garment.

④ Sew the topstitching, sewing until you meet where you started. Sew over three to four of the first stitches to lock the stitching.

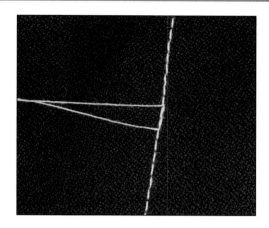

⑤ For two rows of topstitching, use the sewing machine foot as a guide and sew an even distance from the first row of stitches or use a twin needle.

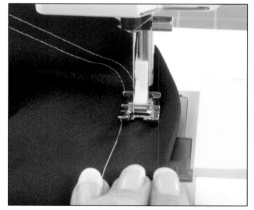

TIP

Lockstitch

Many sewing machines have a lockstitch feature, which allows the machine to sew in one spot to lock the threads. When topstitching, use the lockstitch feature to eliminate overlapped stitching.

Invisible Hems

An invisible hem is the most commonly used hemming technique. The stitches are invisible or at least hidden on the right side of the fabric.

---

1. Prepare the hem as previously described (see p. 148). Anchor a hand-sewing thread in the inside of the hem at a seam allowance.

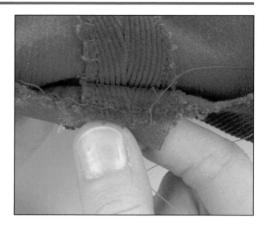

2. Using a catch-stitch, slipstitch, or blind stitch (see p. 37–39), pick up one or two threads of the body of the garment fabric, directly behind the top of the inside edge of the hem allowance.

3. Continue hand sewing until you reach the end, and anchor the thread in the seam allowance or hem.

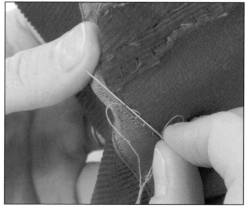

Machine Blind Hems

Many sewing machines have a built-in blind stitch. This stitch can sew a nearly invisible hem.

1 Locate the blind stitch on your sewing machine. Refer to your sewing machine manual for the settings.

2 Prepare the hem as previously described (see p. 148).

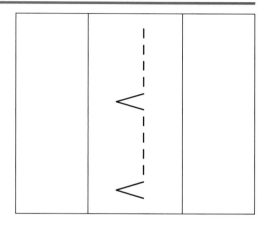

3 Fold the garment back, right sides together, to reveal the inside of the hem edge. Allow the straight stitching of the blind hem to fall on the hem allowance and the swing stitch to barely catch the body of the garment.

Faced Hems

Curved hems and hem extensions are the most common reasons for creating a faced hem. A garment that is too short can suddenly have enough fabric for a hem by adding a faced hem.

1 Mark the hem as previously described (see p. 148). Choose a single-fold bias tape in a width that would make an appropriate hem for your purpose.

2 Unfold the bias tape and place the fold on the hemline where you want the hem to turn up. Trim the fabric to match the edge of the bias tape.

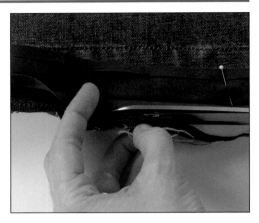

3 Pin the bias tape to the hem edge with the right sides together. Use extra tape at the seams to join the ends of the bias tape.

④ Seam the bias tape to fit the hem area.

⑤ Unfold the bias tape, aligning the edge of the bias tape and the edge of the garment. Sew in the existing fold on the bias tape.

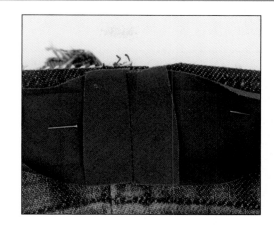

⑥ Grade and under-stitch the seam as described on p. 98 and p. 100 to assist the bias tape in staying to the inside.

⑦ Press the bias tape hem to the inside of the garment. Sew the unattached bias-tape edge to the body of the garment with hand or machine sewing.

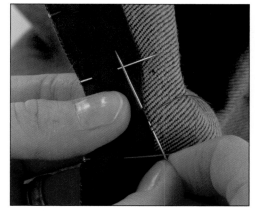

Stretchy hems require stretch stitches to prevent the hem from popping stitches when the fabric is stretched.

Use the stretch and create a lettuce hem by stretching the crossgrain of a knit of bias of a woven fabric while applying a medium-width zigzag stitch to the edge.

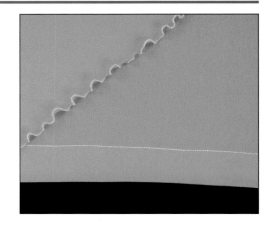

Many sewing machines have a stretch blind stitch and stretch stitches for a topstitched hem.

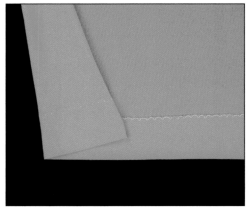

Decorative additions to a hemline can be a planned design detail or used to hide previous hemlines when adding additional length.

A seam line at the hemline, such as using a bias-tape facing, allows you to add lace or piping to the hemline, further extending the length of the garment.

Rickrack and decorative trims can be used to mask a previous hemline when a hem is let down.

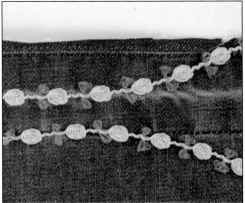

chapter 12

Using a Purchased Pattern

There are a multitude of commercial patterns available to sew clothing, home-décor items, costumes, and so on. Patterns provide guidance to create almost anything. Adding your choice of fabric and notions makes the item what you want it to be. If you're learning how to sew, try one of the many beginner patterns that are available. You can browse through pattern catalogs both online or at fabric stores.

WHERE TO FIND PATTERNS

Your first stop in the fabric store is the pattern catalogs as shown in the photo below. They're divided into sections, so you can focus on the type of pattern you're looking for. The images in the catalog represent the pattern envelope and contain enough information to help you make a decision.

The pattern catalogs and the front of the pattern envelopes show you what a pattern can create. Sometimes you have to use your imagination to see the item that you want.

Most pattern companies also have their catalogs online, so you can browse from the comfort of home and take your time. These sites are also a wealth of information for fitting problems and alterations.

SELECT A PATTERN

Once you find the pattern you want, write down the number and the size.

Patterns are usually in large drawers arranged by pattern manufacturers and pattern numbers. This information is listed on the outside of each drawer.

Once you've found the correct pattern, you'll need to find the correct size. The patterns should be arranged by size but often are out of order because of customers changing their mind and stuffing patterns back into the drawers.

Just as with ready-made clothes, there is no guarantee that the size you normally wear will fit in everything you try on. Because sizes vary among pattern manufacturers, the size charts may not perfectly match your body measurements. In this section, you'll learn what measurements are important for what you want to sew so you go home with the pattern size you need.

Before you purchase a pattern, know your measurements. Use the size charts from the pattern company and your measurements to choose your correct pattern size. Don't automatically purchase the size you normally wear in ready-made garments.

Use the **bust measurement** as a guide to choose a pattern size for tops, dresses, blouses, jackets, and coats.

Use the **waist measurement** as a guide to choose a pattern size for skirts that are not fitted in the hip area.

Use the **hip measurement** as a guide to choose a pattern size for pants and fitted skirts.

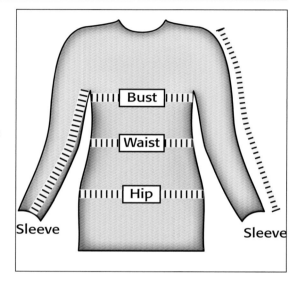

Length measurements are important, but if the envelope measurements are in the ballpark, they can be adjusted on the pattern before you lay out and cut out the pattern. Adjustment lines are printed on almost all patterns to adjust the length of garments. Lengthening and shortening is not done at the bottom of an area as in hemming ready-made garments.

The information you need to successfully achieve sewing a pattern starts on the envelope.

The front of the envelope shows the completed pattern (for example, a garment) in different views. The letter or number assigned to each view is a guide for which pattern pieces and directions you'll be following. The pattern number and size(s) in that envelope are also on the front of the envelope as many patterns are multi-sized.

The back of the pattern envelope tells you the suggested fabrics, the notions you need, how much fabric you'll need for the view you choose, how many pattern pieces are inside the envelope, and so on. Use the back of the envelope as a guide. If you'll be adding a lot of length to a garment, you'll need more fabric than is listed on the envelope chart.

Read the entire envelope to be sure you're buying everything you need for all parts of a garment.

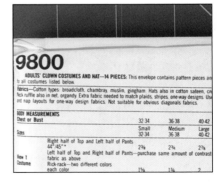

9800

ADULTS' CLOWN COSTUMES AND HAT—14 PIECES: This envelope contains pattern pieces and to all costumes listed below.

Fabrics—Cotton types: broadcloth, chambray, muslin, gingham. Hats also in cotton sateen, chintz. Neck ruffle also in net, organdy. Extra fabric needed to match plaids, stripes, one-way designs. Use with nap layouts for one-way design fabrics. Not suitable for obvious diagonals fabrics.

BODY MEASUREMENTS

Chest or Bust		32-34	36-38	40-42
Sizes		Small	Medium	Large
		32-34	36-38	40-42
New 1 Costume	Right half of Top and Left half of Pants 44"/45"**	2⅝	2¾	2⅞
	Left half of Top and Right half of Pants—purchase same amount of contrast fabric as above			
	Rick-rack—two different colors each color	1⅝	1¾	2

I always have to return to the fabric store for something I forgot to buy. Is there a way to avoid a second trip?

One trick is to use a highlighter to mark the items that you need or all the parts of the view that you'll be making on the envelope. Many pattern envelopes can be viewed on the Internet via pattern manufacturers' Web sites; you can use these sites to make printouts at home and make a list before you go shopping.

Inside the Envelope

A pattern envelope is usually stuffed with pattern pieces. Start with the instruction sheet. It will tell you which tissue pieces you need for the view you're making as well as the layout and sewing directions.

GENERAL DIRECTIONS

The instruction sheet has a general directions area, which will explain symbols and basic construction information. Take the time to read through the sheet the first time you're using a pattern.

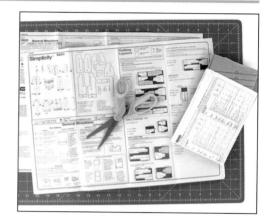

THE PATTERN PIECES

The instruction sheet will show you which pattern pieces you'll need for the view you're sewing.

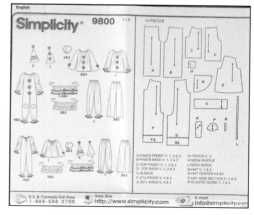

The instruction sheet pieces shown are labeled:

A-PANTS FRONT V. 1, 2 & 3
B-PANTS BACK V. 1, 2 & 3
C-TOP FRONT V. 1, 2 & 3
D- TOP BACK V. 1, 2 & 3
E-SLEEVE
F (F1)-FRONT V. 4 & 5
G (G1)- BACK V. 4 & 5
H- PATCH V. 4
K-NECK RUFFLE
L-NECK GUIDE
M-HAT V. 1 & 3
N-HAT CENTER V2 &3
P-HAT SIDE SECTION V. 2 & 3
R-ELASTIC GUIDE V. 2 & 3

Simplicity® 9800 1/4 14 PIECES

U.S. & Canada Toll-Free 1-888-588-2700
Web Site http://www.simplicity.com
E-mail info@simplicity.com

After you've selected the correct pattern pieces for your project, you'll need to do the following steps before you start to sew.

① Separate and cut out the pieces using scissors that you only use to cut paper. Cut notches out beyond the seam allowance rather than into the seam allowance to preserve the full seam allowance when you cut out the fabric.

② Press the pattern pieces smooth with a lukewarm dry iron.

③ After you've located the layout guide for the view and width of fabric you're using, press and lay out the preshrunk fabric as it is in the layout guide.

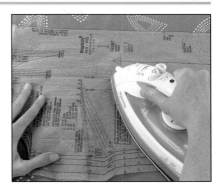

④ Make any adjustments that you may need to the pattern following the guidelines in the instruction sheet. The photo shows lines that are used to lengthen or shorten the garment. These lines are to be cut and an even amount of paper is either inserted or removed between the lines to lengthen or shorten the pattern respectively. This adjustment must also be done to any other pieces to which the adjusted piece will be attached.

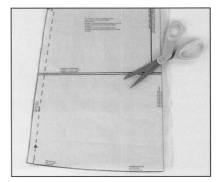

TIP

Use the Same Pattern for Multiple Sizes

Preserve multi-sized patterns by tracing the pattern size you need onto lightweight interfacing or pattern tracing paper. Be sure to transfer all the pattern markings and label the pieces. Continue to use this method each time you need to make the pattern in different sizes.

Lay Out the Pattern

Laying out the pattern pieces correctly is the first step to having them fit together and hang properly in the finished garment. This step usually requires a large, flat working surface. Anyplace where the pattern and fabric can be laid out flat will work.

Lay out and smooth the pattern pieces on the fabric to closely resemble the diagram on the guide sheet.

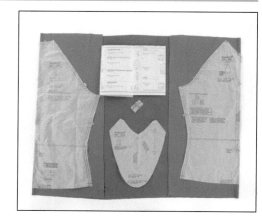

The grain line and on the fold lines are the first area of the pattern pieces to be pinned down to the fabric. (See p. 50 for grain line information.)

A pattern piece that is laid out on the fold needs the edge of the pattern piece to follow the fold for the entire length of the pattern piece.

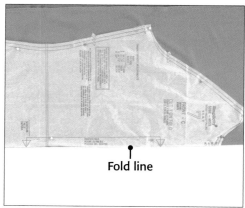

Fold line

Grain line markings on pattern pieces are straight lines, usually with arrows on the ends. The length of the grain line marking varies with the size of the pattern piece.

The distance between the selvedge or the fold of the fabric and the grain line should be the same for the entire length of the grain line. It is not enough for it to *look* straight—it must *be* straight for the finished garment to hang properly.

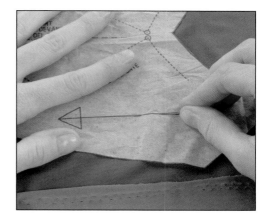

Working from the pinned-down grain line, smooth the pattern pieces so they're perfectly flat on the fabric.

Pin so that the pattern pieces are held securely in place but the pins will not interfere with the edge cutting lines. The pins should also lay flat without bunching the fabric or the pattern piece.

FAQ

My fabric will show the pinholes. How can I cut the fabric without using pins?
You can purchase pattern weights to weight down the pattern pieces in place instead of pins. Many people use an assortment of metal washers—just be sure they're oil-free so they won't stain your fabric.

Sharp scissors are essential to cutting out a pattern! Scissors must cut without shredding the fabric so that you can cut accurately. Working on the same flat surface that the pattern was laid out on will contribute to keeping the cutting accurate and prevent the pattern pieces from shifting.

You should use scissors that will glide along the table, such as dressmaker's shears, which are preferable to cut out a pattern.

You'll follow the edge of the pattern pieces by cutting to the outside edge of the line for the size you're using.

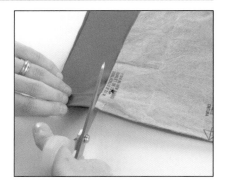

Cut single and double notches beyond the seam allowance to preserve the entire seam allowance.

The only area that is not cut is any pattern line that, per the pattern layout directions, is set on a fold of fabric.

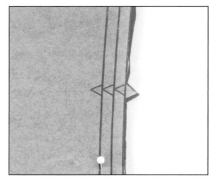

There are dots and lines on the pattern pieces that must be transferred to the fabric for construction purposes. These markings will help fit the pattern pieces together properly. In this section, a dressmaker's carbon and a tracing tool are used in the example. See Chapter 2, "Marking Fabric," for additional methods to transfer pattern markings.

Always test your marking for removability on a scrap piece of fabric *before* you mark the cut-out fabric. Using a color for marking that is barely visible is advisable, just in case it can't be completely removed from the test sample.

Dressmaker's carbon, used with a tracing wheel, is placed between the layers of fabric after the pattern is cut out so that the marking is on the wrong side of the fabric. This process allows the markings to be transferred exactly as they are printed on the pattern pieces.

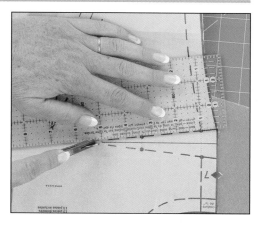

When you're transferring long, straight lines, such as darts, the tracing wheel should follow a straight edge to keep the markings accurate.

Cross the lines to form an X at the center of dots.

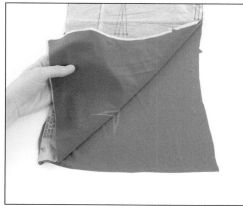

chapter **13**

Adding Pizzazz

Sure, you can put pieces together to sew a seam, but making a garment or home-décor item in your own style is what makes sewing fun and creative. Special seams, trim added to seams, and embellishment are all ways to add a touch of color, create your own look, and make a splash with something that might otherwise be plain.

Flat felled seams are most commonly found in jeans. They're a highly visible seam with a sporty appearance.

---

① Sew the seam with the wrong sides of the fabric together so that the seam allowance is on the right side of the fabric.

② Press the seam open as it was sewn, and then press the seam to one side.

③ Trim the seam allowance that is on the bottom to approximately ⅛ inch from the seam line.

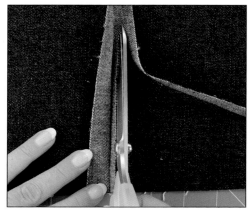

4 Fold and press the wide seam allowance in half wrong sides together, folding the raw edge under to meet the seam line. Then press folded seam allowance over to cover trimmed seam allowance as shown in the photo on the right.

5 Using the presser foot as a guide and adjusting the needle position, if possible, topstitch close to the folded edge.

6 Press the entire seam.

TIP

If the folded seam allowance wants to twist or slip out of place, take the time to baste it in place before machine topstitching.

French seams enclose the seam allowance within the seam to have a perfectly smooth seam allowance that will not fray or attract balls of lint. Sheer fabric is an excellent choice to use with French seams because the seam finish will show through this type of fabric.

1 To create a seam that will total a ⅝-inch seam allowance, sew a scant ½-inch seam with the wrong sides of the fabric together.

2 Press the seam to one side.

3 Trim both the seam allowances to ⅛ inch.

4. Fold the right sides of the fabric together along the sewn seam.

5. Press the right sides of the fabric together, setting (pressing) the folded seam edge.

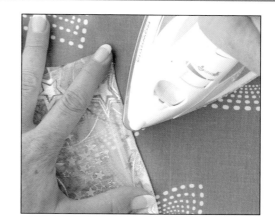

6. Sew ⅛ inch from the fold line to enclose the trimmed seam.

7. Press the seam as it was sewn and then to one side.

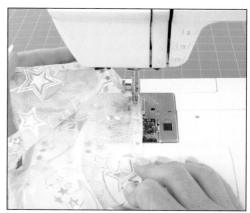

TIP

You can create sheer curtain panels that are wide enough for any window by joining lengths of fabric using French seams. The seams will look like decorative finishes rather than uninspired hems on the sides of panels.

Adding details such as trim and cording can add dimension and flair to anything you sew. Use trim to accentuate a subdued color in a print by choosing the color you want to bring to the forefront.

Additions to seams are sewn to one layer before the seam is sewn. Keep the stitching within the seam allowance with the decorative part of the trim toward the body of the fabric.

Bulky additions such as cording are sewn with a cording foot or zipper foot, sewing the cording to one layer of the fabric first.

When sewing the final seam with the fabric's right sides together and the cording sandwiched in between, use the stitching that attached the trim as a guide. This enables you to be sure you're sewing the seam so it will enclose the stitching that attached the trim.

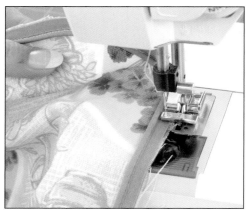

Curved seams must have gathered or bias trim. Flat trims will not bend with the curved edge and will cause the item to curl rather than lay flat.

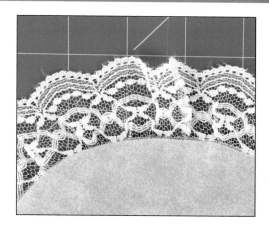

Corners and turns in seams may require the seam allowance area of the trim to be clipped or notched so that the turn can be made and the trim will lie smoothly (see p. 73).

Trim can be added to disguise wear lines when letting down a hem (see p. 159). If you're adding a facing hem, attach the trim before closing the facing.

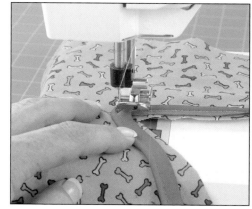

TIP

Preshrink Cording and Trim

Preshrink trims the same way you would your fabric. Place them in a laundry bag or nylon stocking to keep them from tangling in the laundering process.

Make Your Own Cording

Cording is available in the home décor section of fabric stores, but the stores may not have what you had in mind for a project. This section will show you how to create your own cording.

Always preshrink the cording. It should have the same laundering instructions as the fabric that you will use with it.

1. Choose the size cording you want.

2. Measure around the cording with a tape measure and include a seam allowance on each side of the cording. This measurement will be used to calculate the width of bias strips you'll need to cut.

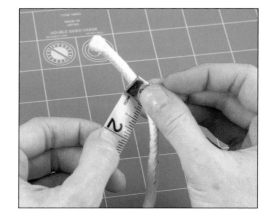

3. Cut bias strips of fabric the width you'll need to cover the cording.

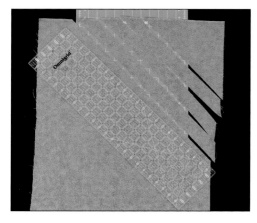

④ Join strips by placing them right sides together, forming a V. Align the edges so they match at the desired seam allowance stitching line.

⑤ Join enough strips together to cover the length of cording you need.

⑥ Press the seams open to distribute the bulk that the seams may create.

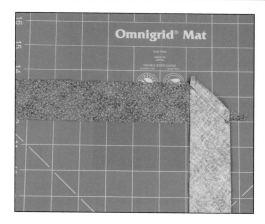

⑦ Wrap the bias strip around the cording, maintaining the bias of the fabric. Use a zipper foot to sew the cording closed.

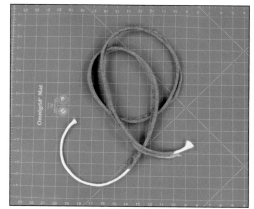

TIP

Coordinate Pillows

For a one-of-a-kind design, buy two different fabrics: one to sew the body of the pillow and one to create your own cording. Save scraps of fabric from curtains and make cording for your pillows to coordinate the room.

Trim with Decorative Stitching

Experiment with the stitches on your sewing machine that you might not otherwise use to create an attractive decorative trim.

Test the density of various decorative stitches on your sewing machine to obtain the amount of color you want.

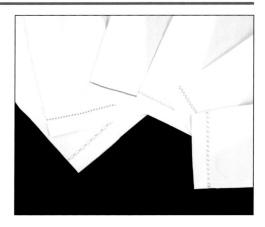

There are a wide variety of threads available. Decorative threads, such as polyester and rayon, will shine when used with decorative stitches. Variegated threads have different repeat patterns. Depending on the repeat in the thread and the density of the stitch you're sewing, you can achieve different looks.

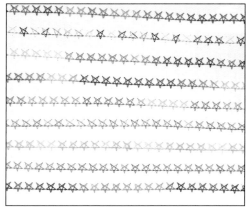

The density of many embroidered stitches may pucker and pull the fabric. Starching the fabric may solve the problem. Lightweight fabrics can be made thicker by using stabilizers. Temporary spray adhesives will hold the stabilizer to the fabric.

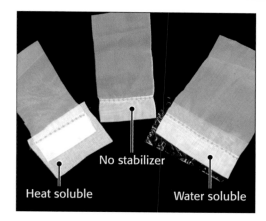

No stabilizer

Heat soluble

Water soluble

Prevent stabilizers from being seen by using vanishing stabilizers that will dissolve in water or vanish from the heat of an iron, so the stabilizer will disappear in the finished product.

Bobbin thread is lighter weight than other threads. Using bobbin thread in embroidery prevents a bulky backside. Use a color that matches the fabric to make the embroidery almost invisible on the back side.

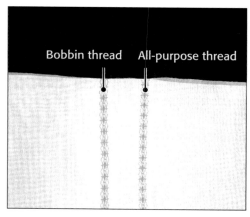

Bobbin thread   All-purpose thread

TIP

Seam Guides

When you're sewing decorative stitches, the machine needle is moving from side to side. Do not watch the needle because it will not help you keep the stitches straight. Train yourself to watch a seam guide, not the machine needle.

Sew on Badges or Appliqués

Some ready-made badges and appliqués have a plastic backing that adheres when ironed onto fabric; however many launderings and heavy wear will dictate that they should be sewn into place. A badge is used in the photos shown here.

Hand sewing, from the back side of the badge to the right side of the fabric, using small stitches around the entire edge of the badge or appliqué, as shown, will hold it in place.

Machine sewing is done with a matching thread color, sewing as close to the edge of the badge as possible. You can use clear nylon thread to make the stitching less obvious.

TIP

Holding a Badge in Place

The thickness of a badge may bend pins and make it impossible to pin in place. If the badge doesn't have a plastic backing that melts with the heat of an iron, try a temporary basting spray to keep it in place while you sew.

Special Machines

Once you start sewing, you're bound to notice different types of stitching on ready-made clothing and wonder how those stitches were created. Beyond the stitches on a basic sewing machine, the options are endless. The decision to invest in the various types of equipment that is available is a personal choice. Visit local sewing machine dealers and discover the latest technological advances before you make a decision.

SERGER/OVERLOCK MACHINES

Sergers, sometimes referred to as overlock machines, trim the fabric and apply threads to enclose the edge of the fabric in one step. They use from two to eight threads at the same time as they sew. Varying the number of threads, the number of and position of machine needles, and the machine settings dictates the number of stitches the machine is capable of sewing.

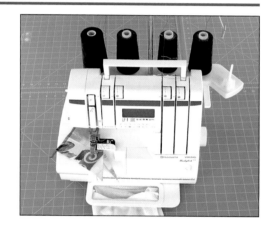

MACHINE EMBROIDERY

Machine embroidery has expanded well beyond built-in decorative stitches. Home sewing machines are capable of stitching designs that open a new world of thread artistry. Special hooping techniques, combined with purchased designs or digitized designs, have endless possibilities. Increasing your knowledge of the different types of software that is available can expand your decorative options.

chapter 14

Problem Solving

Sewing can be a very enjoyable hobby. But when you feel like you're spending most of your time fighting with your sewing machine, have no fear. Your sewing machine doesn't have to be your worst enemy. In this chapter, you'll learn why sewing problems happen and how to solve them when they occur.

Basic Sewing Machine Troubleshooting

As with anything related to your sewing machine, your sewing machine manual is the best resource for solving machine problems. If you don't have your manual, the following checklist can help you solve many different types of problems.

- **Rethread the sewing machine.** Always thread the sewing machine with the presser foot up. Make sure that the thread is running through all the guides on the machine. See p. 16.

- **Rethread the bobbin case.** You should use the correct bobbin for your sewing machine. When threading the bobbin, it needs to be evenly wound. After the bobbin is in place, the thread must go through all of the guides. Still having problems? Flip the bobbin over so the thread is feeding off the bobbin from a different direction. See p. 12

- **Change your needle.** Is the needle worn or bent? The sewing machine needle should be changed at any sign of stitch problems. Be sure to use a needle that is appropriate for the fabric and thread that you're using. An incorrect type of needle can cause sewing machine problems and fraying thread. Refer to your sewing machine manual to know the proper way to replace a sewing machine needle and the proper kind of needle for your machine.

Note: *Avoid bent needles by allowing the feed dog to feed the fabric under the presser foot. Never push or pull the fabric while the machine is running.*

- **Check the placement of your sewing machine needle.** The needle should be seated properly all the way up so that the thread follows the groove in the needle because the needle must work in unison with the bobbin thread.

- **Clean and oil your machine.** Regular removal of lint and oiling as instructed in your manual are important to keeping a sewing machine functioning properly. Follow the machine care information in your sewing machine manual.

Note: *If you don't have your sewing machine manual, see p.11 or p. 198 for how you might be able to get a copy.*

FAQ

How do I know if it's worthwhile to have my machine repaired or if I should just buy a new one?

Find a reputable sewing machine repair shop and get an estimate on how much it will cost to repair your machine. Sewing guilds and fabric stores can usually lead you to reputable repair shops. Consider if the advanced options on a new sewing machine would be more helpful to you with your sewing project than your old machine. Then make your decision.

There are times when your sewing machine produces stitches that do not look the way you want them to look. This section will help you determine how you can fix the problem. You can also refer to your manual to learn how to make the correct adjustments to your machine.

INCORRECT TENSION SETTINGS

The photo on the right shows what can result from incorrect tension settings. Before you change the tension settings:

- Check to make sure you're using the correct needle.

- Be sure that the machine is properly threaded, both the upper threading and the bobbin. Always thread the machine with the presser foot up so that the upper tension regulator is released and it accepts the thread.

- Test that the tension discs are engaging by putting the presser foot down and gently pulling the needle thread to the rear of the machine. You should feel a difference in resistance between when the presser foot is down and when it is up.

TIP

Remove Incorrect Stitching

As tempting as it may be to just stitch over problem stitches, take the time to remove loops and tangles before you continue sewing. You'll have stronger stitches in the end and less chance of the malfunctioning stitches creating more problems.

SKIPPED STITCHES

Skipped stitches are usually related to a needle problem. Changing the type of needle if you're sewing a different kind of fabric will solve the problem. If you've been sewing the same fabric and start skipping stitches, the needle may be bent and should be changed.

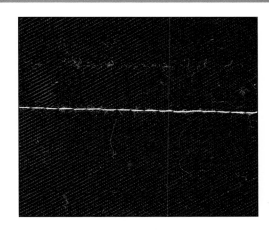

HOLES IN THE FABRIC

Holes and snags that appear between the stitches in the fabric are caused by the needle shaft being too thick for the fabric you're sewing. Change to a smaller needle and a different type of point on the needle to solve the problem.

CONTINUED ON NEXT PAGE

JAMMING STITCHES

This common problem has simple solutions. If your machine sews in one spot and no stitches are forming or if it won't go forward after you finish backstitching, try these problem solvers.

- If the problem happens every time you backstitch, consider having a scrap of fabric butted to the end of the seam. Trim away the scrap after you've sewn the seam.

- Clean the lint out of the machine regularly. A buildup of lint in the bobbin area of the machine can prevent the feed dogs from moving forward.

- Rethreading your machine with the presser foot up and follow the instructions in your machine manual.

- Replace the sewing needle.

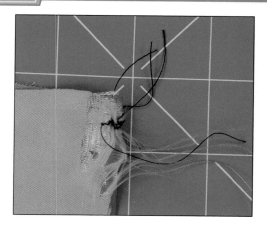

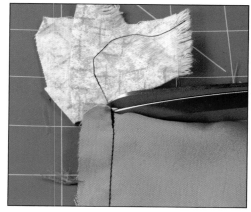

PUCKERS IN THE FABRIC

Puckered stitches can be solved by adjusting the stitch length to a longer stitch length. If that fails or you're using shear, silky, or slippery fabric, sew the fabric with a layer of gift wrapping tissue paper or stabilizer holding the fabric taut front and back.

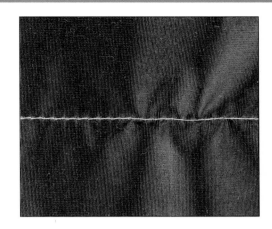

LOOPING THREAD

Almost anyone who has ever operated a sewing machine has experienced sewing a machine stitch and the bobbin thread just creates long loops of thread. This certainly doesn't create a strong stitch. Surprisingly, the problem is usually the upper threading. Refer to the list on p. 188–189 or you can also try turning the spool of thread occasionally so it's coming off the spool in a different direction.

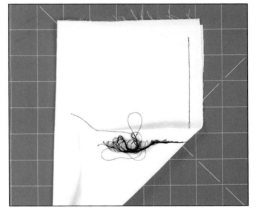

If your machine starts making clunking noises, don't panic, but do stop sewing. Sewing machines have a lot of moving parts, so problems can happen. Consider the noise as a warning and prevent damage by stopping to check things out.

- Did you thread the machine just before the noises started? If so, double-check that you've threaded the machine correctly.

- Is the bobbin seated properly and is it the correct bobbin for your sewing machine? Rethread with the correct bobbin.

- Is the needle bent or worn and all the way up in proper position? Replace the needle any time you're in doubt.

- Has the machine been cleaned and lint removed regularly? Those noises may be a reminder that you're jamming the feeders with lint. Stop and clean the machine.

- If you have tried all of the above and your machine is still making unusual noises, take it to a repair shop. A gear or part may have loosened or it may need another type of repair.

Separating Fabric

A seam that allows the fabric to separate, leaving a gap between the two sides, is probably not going to be very strong. Here are some ways to make your stitches more durable.

- Shorten the stitch length. Smaller stitches may draw the fabric tighter together.

- Apply more pressure to the presser foot to hold the fabric tighter in place. This adjustment should be explained in your machine manual.

- Are the upper thread and bobbin thread even in the seam? Adjust the thread tension as described in your sewing machine manual.

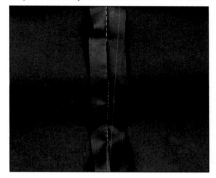

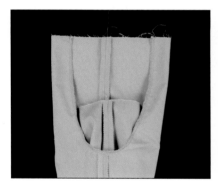

TIP

How to Avoid Popped Crotch Seams on Pants

Sew both legs first and then sew the entire crotch seam to join the legs. Sew again ⅛ inch inside the first row of stitching on the seam allowance to reinforce the seam. Trim the seam and apply a seam finish to keep the seam strong through many launderings.

It may seem difficult to thread a sewing machine needle because the needle is stationery. However, you can use some of the same easy methods as you would for threading a hand-sewing needle.

- White behind the needle makes the eye of the needle easier to see. Painting the area of the presser foot shank behind a sewing machine needle with corrective fluid like you might use to correct a printed typo makes seeing the needle eye easier.
- Before you thread the needle, cut the thread at an angle with sharp scissors.
- Use a needle threader (see p. 32).
- Stiffen the thread with beeswax or saliva.

Note: *Many new sewing machines have an automatic needle threader option, and some sewing machine companies offer handheld sewing machine needle threaders. Visit local sewing machine dealers to find what's available for your sewing machine.*

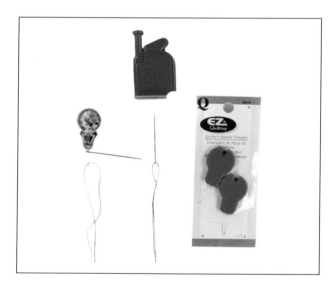

Pieces that Do Not Fit Together

Almost everything you sew is going to require that you sew pieces together. Having the pieces sewn together properly will affect the final fit and appearance of the garment.

- Fitting pieces together starts at the layout and cutting stage. If the fabric and pattern are not smooth when you're laying them out, the pieces will be distorted from the desired shape and size (see p. 168).

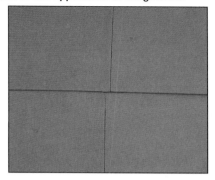

- Sewing accurate and consistent seam allowances affects the size of pieces as you continue to join pieces. A ⅛-inch difference may not seem like a big difference until you've sewn six panels of a skirt, with ⅜-inch seams instead of the ⅝-inch seams as needed for the pattern. This can affect the size of a waistband, causing it not to fit properly.

- Some pieces need to be eased in order for them to fit together. Easing is done with rows of basting stitches to draw the edges of the fabric closer together. Easing doesn't have any tucks or gathers (see p. 80).

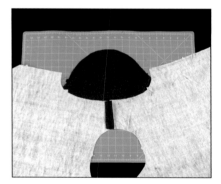

TIP

Use a tape measure and check the seam guides to be sure they're accurate. Remember that if you change the needle position of your sewing machine, the seam guide will be affected.

You can purchase a manual or a copy of a manual for almost any older machine from sources other than the manufacturer (see p. 11). The following list is a source to purchase manuals directly from sewing machine manufacturers. Have your machine's model number handy, if possible, when trying to track down a manual.

Manufacturers		
Company	*Web site*	*Phone*
Baby Lock–Tacony	www.babylock.com	800-422-2952
Bernina USA	www.berninausa.com	800-405-2739
Brother Company	www.brother.com	800-284-4357
Elna	www.elna.com	800-848-3562
Husquavarna Viking	www.husqvarnaviking.com	800-446-2333
Janome	www.janome.com	800-631-0183
Pfaff	www.pfaff.com	800-997-3233
Riccar	www.riccar.com	800-995-9110
Sears Kenmore	www.kenmore.com	800-366-7278
Simplicity Sewing Machines	www.simplicitysewing.com	800-822-6691
Singer Company	www.singerco.com	800-474-6437
White Sewing Machines	www.whitesewing.com	800-446-2333

Test the Fiber Content

Many bargain tables and fabric remnants do not have the bolt end information that tells you the fabric's fiber content. Don't despair—you can get a good idea of what the fibers are by doing a burn test, which will help you know how to care for the fabric.

No special equipment is needed to do a burn test. Always use caution and have water readily available when doing a burn test.

Hold a small piece of fabric with tweezers over a sink. Gently bring a match flame to the edge of the scrap of fabric, and pay attention to the smell when the fiber burns.

Burn Test	
Fiber	*Burn Results*
Acetate or triacetate	Catches the flame and burns quickly. The melt of the fibers is a brittle, black bead. Produces a vinegar odor.
Acrylic	Catches the flame and burns quickly, producing a sputtering flame. The melted fibers are hard, black, irregular beads. Produces a bitter, irritating odor.
Cotton or linen	As soon as they make contact with the flame, these fibers burn. They burn very quickly and leave a light, wispy ash. Produces an odor like burning paper.
Nylon	Burns evenly with a blue and orange flame. Melts into a hard, gray-brown to black bead. Produces a celery odor.
Polyester	Burns with an orange flame and sputters as it burns. The melt produces a shiny, hard, round bead. Produces a sweet odor.
Rayon	Burns quickly and leaves a very slight ash. Produces an odor similar to burning leaves.
Silk	Usually burns, but not with a steady flame. Produces an ash that is easily crumbled. Produces an odor similar to singed hair.
Wool	Produces a steady flame but is difficult to keep burning. Produces an odor similar to singed hair.

Index